HELL'S KITCHEN

BEHIND THE DREAM

An imprint of Penguin Random House LLC
1745 Broadway, New York, NY 10019
penguinrandomhouse.com

This book was produced by Melcher Media, Inc.
melcher.com

Founder and CEO: Charles Melcher
Vice President and COO: Bonnie Eldon
Editorial Director: Lauren Nathan
Production Director: Susan Lynch
Executive Editor: Christopher Steighner
Senior Editor: Megan Worman
Assistant Editor: Madison Brown
Editorial Assistant: Sonia Menken
Editorial Intern: Grace Luckett

Book design by Morcos Key (Jon Key, Ana Valeria Castillos)
Additional editorial contributions by Camille Kellogg

Thanks also to Amélie Cherlin and Laura Wallis.

LIBRARY OF CONGRESS CATALOGING-IN-PUBLICATION DATA
has been applied for.

ISBN 9798217176809 (hardcover)

ISBN 9798217176816 (ebook)

Printed in China

10 9 8 7 6 5 4 3 2 1

The authorized representative in the EU for product safety and compliance is Penguin Random House Ireland, Morrison Chambers, 32 Nassau Street, Dublin D02 YH68, Ireland.

https://eu-contact.penguin.ie.

HELL'S KITCHEN

BEHIND THE DREAM

THE OFFICIAL BOOK FROM

ALICIA KEYS

WRITTEN BY LISE FUNDERBURG

TABLE OF CONTENTS

1

BEGINNINGS

This page: The theater district in 2005
Previous page: Maleah Joi Moon as Ali in the opening scene of *Hell's Kitchen*

THE SPARK

Alicia Keys

The main spark for *Hell's Kitchen* was frustration, because in the early 2000s, what I was seeing on Broadway and television and film was quite distant from life as I knew it. It was annoying. I kept wondering, *Where are the stories of people that I know?* To be clear, I'm not just talking about Black people, but I am talking about theater being more diverse. There should also be brown people, Asian people, differently colored people who have unique stories and voices that aren't generalized and stereotyped. Obviously, that was a while ago, it was pre-*Hamilton*, and I do truly feel that things have evolved from that spot. But coupled with the frustration I felt at that time, people were asking me, "Would you write a musical? Would you do a musical film?" I thought, *I guess, but how, when, where?* I didn't know how that would start or what that would look like.

One glimmer of a way forward came from *Stick Fly*, Lydia Diamond's play about a Black family on Martha's Vineyard, which debuted on Broadway in 2011. Alicia composed the incidental music for the play, which took on issues of class, race, and gender.

Stick Fly was riveting. The way it communicated what the family was going through and feeling—I had never seen anything like that before. That was around the same time I founded my company, AKW Productions. The slogan of AKW is "the business of inspiration." Through film, television, theater, and music, I wanted to create diverse stories, preferably stories you haven't quite seen and haven't quite heard. They'd give a different perspective, something that makes you realize, *Wow, I never looked at it like that before.*

One day, it landed on me that Manhattan Plaza, where I grew up, was the richest soil for this kind of story. Thinking about Manhattan Plaza and my experience there brought me to what a unique neighborhood Hell's Kitchen is, which brought me to all the different people that I knew there. I was also thinking about what success is or feels like or should be. It took me a long time to have a healthy relationship with success. A lot of times I would find myself in rooms and feel like, *I don't even know why I'm here. How did I even get here?*

All of that together created the desire to tell this story of this girl, this building, this community. From day one, I was very clear that you would see the main character only in the seventeenth year of her life. It would not go beyond that. You had a sense, *Man, something is brewing*, but you had no idea what would come. I wanted to focus on the very everyday yet special experience of this girl with this unheard story, and that was the spark that started the dream.

THE (REAL) ROOTS OF THAT UNHEARD STORY

It makes sense that many theatergoers come to *Hell's Kitchen* expecting a storyline that perfectly parallels Alicia Keys's childhood. In fact, it's only loosely based on her experiences growing up in NYC: In the show, as in Alicia's life, a single mother and her daughter live on Manhattan's West Side. The mother is white and the father is Black, and the mother does everything she can to protect her strong-willed child from harm. It's the 1990s; the neighborhood is debilitated by drugs and prostitution, but it's also a place where people watch out for each other and family can be built and chosen.

Beyond these foundations, Alicia and seventeen-year-old Ali, the protagonist of the show, have countless differences in the details of their lives: Alicia actually began learning piano a decade earlier than Ali, for example, and Alicia's father was not a jazz musician. Still, they share concerns for community, artistry, identity, love, and becoming. Alicia wasn't interested in staging an autobiography but, at the same time, she recognized that she had a well of experiences the show could draw upon, starting with the story of her mother, Terria (Terri) Joseph.

Manhattan Plaza in 2006

Alicia Keys
My mom came to New York from Toledo, Ohio, at nineteen. She came to attend New York University [NYU], and she was very excited. She had grown up in a super small town, and coming to New York to study theater and acting and dancing was a big dream.

Terria graduated from NYU in 1971 and enmeshed herself in the city's theater scene. As an emerging artist she struggled to make ends meet, so when an innovative affordable housing project opened up, she set her sights on living there—even though it was in Hell's Kitchen, a downtrodden neighborhood between the Midtown theater district and the Hudson River. Manhattan Plaza consisted of two residential towers that were designated specifically for artists, senior citizens, and people who already lived in the neighborhood. But mostly artists.

Terria Joseph
I had to work really hard to get in there. I did all the paperwork, and thought, *Oh, I'm next*. Everybody was getting apartments, but they must have lost my application. They didn't know me from Adam's tomcat. But in 1978, a year after it opened, they finally gave me the last studio on the top floor of the Tenth Avenue building.

A few years later, Terria was in a casual relationship with a flight attendant named Craig Cook, and when their birth control failed, she became pregnant. Terria knew Craig wasn't ready to be a father. She briefly considered terminating the pregnancy but decided that she could manage raising the child on her own. As she has said, "When people want to come through, they come through."

Terria Joseph
Up until this point, I had been temping as a paralegal. My good friend Alicia, who had all kinds of jobs, including being a Playboy Bunny, was doing the hiring for a law firm. She said, "We've got a big case coming up. You can get all the hours you want, all kinds of overtime." I had just told her I was pregnant. She

said, "You gotta save your money now." We did a little behind-the-scenes mischief, and she got me a job. My Alicia was named after her.

Terria raised her daughter on paralegal wages and made a home for her in Manhattan Plaza (eventually moving from the studio apartment to a one-bedroom), where Terria would live for a total of twenty-six years. Terria worked—a lot—and continued to pursue acting roles when she could, but she dedicated most of her time and resources to her daughter.

Terria Joseph
I used to take Alicia to classes to keep her busy. I was always taking her somewhere. She went to gymnastics, but I had to take her out because she was afraid to flip over. For quite a while, Alicia would get up at 6:30 to swim with Manhattan Plaza's swim team. At some point she said, "Mom, I want to sleep a little later before I go to school." I said, "You got it." It wasn't about torturing her.

Hell's Kitchen abuts Times Square, which at the time was chockablock with porn theaters and peep shows and had no shortage of sketchy characters. Not the easiest place to raise a kid.

Terria Joseph
I went everywhere with her until she got savvy. When she was nine or ten, I asked her to take me to her dance class. She had to take me every step of the way. I acted like I didn't know how much money it was, like I didn't know what a red light was. I said, "Is this where it is?" She said, "Oh, you're so stupid." I said, "I just want to know that you really know. The only way I'll know is if you take me and I act like a dumbbell." Years later, I made Alicia's boyfriend sit with me in our living room and have a conversation, and then I took a little picture of him. I said, "In case she never comes home, at least I can show the police what you look like."

You don't know how things are going to turn out for your kids. She began piano at seven years old, but at one point, she wanted to stop lessons. I said, "Well, I'm paid up until a couple of months from now, so not until you work out that payment plan." Of course, she'd forgotten about it by the time that came. I talked about it with her piano teacher, Margaret Pine, a really nice person who lived in the building and taught her everything in the beginning. Margaret said, "Please don't let her stop. She has a talent and a musicality." So I figured it was worth a try to keep her in that. I was trying to find out what her muse was, and I thought, *That's the best I can do*. I didn't know what else to do besides give her all the chances I could, keep her close to home, and keep her busy so she didn't get involved in some crazy group or something. And it worked out pretty good.

Alicia Keys and her mother, Terria Joseph, at Alicia's high school graduation in 1998

One way Terria kept Alicia close to home was to enroll her in the Professional Performing Arts School (PPAS), which is only four blocks north of Manhattan Plaza. At PPAS, Alicia met a music teacher who would have an extraordinary impact on her life: the composer, pianist, and vocalist Aziza Miller.

Alicia Keys
I remember the first time I walked into the room and saw Miss Aziza. It was breathtaking. I felt like, *Whoa. That's me*. I recognized something of myself in her.

Aziza Miller, Alicia's high school music teacher
I heard Alicia sing at a school concert when she was probably thirteen. She had a solo, and I said, "Oh, wow." It was more than someone with a good voice. I saw her soul. That's the only way I can say it. I saw her soul. She showed me who she really was. She didn't know it, but she did.

A year or so later, Alicia came to PPAS and into my class. Alicia was always curious about learning. She was driven about wanting to go somewhere with music. It wasn't just a phase for her. It was similar to what I felt from the time I was five years old. I recognized the passion in her, because it was the same thing that I had. I wanted to nurture that talent and curiosity about chords and structure and notation and harmonization and conducting.

I taught all my students music theory, and it was something that she flourished in. I must say that I was

MANHATTAN PLAZA

At the top of the first act, Ali introduces the audience to her world. "Me and my mother—yeah, that's my mother—live on the forty-second floor of a forty-four-story building on Forty-Third Street between Ninth and Tenth Avenues, right in the heart of the neighborhood some people know as Hell's Kitchen." The location is real, as is the building, and it was Alicia Keys's actual childhood home (although she and her mother, actress Terria Joseph, had less of a view from the eleventh floor). The mother and daughter lived in the famous Manhattan Plaza complex, which is known by some as "Broadway's Bedroom," both for its proximity to the city's theater district and for the number of its residents who are involved in the creative and performing arts.

The plaza's two towers were originally intended to invigorate a down-and-out tenement neighborhood with market-rate housing apartments, but midway through construction, it fell into financial difficulties. The way out was through an innovative approach to federally subsidized affordable housing: Not only were rents adjusted according to tenant incomes, but 70% of the apartments were earmarked for people in the arts, 15% to low-income neighborhood residents, and 15% to senior citizens. The result was—and still is—a vibrant creative community, where, as Ali says, "you never know what you're going to hear when the elevator doors open up."

FAMOUS RESIDENTS OF MANHATTAN PLAZA

JANE ALEXANDER
TIMOTHÉE CHALAMET
LARRY DAVID
PATRICK DEMPSEY
COLMAN DOMINGO
GIANCARLO ESPOSITO
TERRENCE HOWARD
ANGELA LANSBURY
AL PACINO
TENNESSEE WILLIAMS

Alicia Keys and her piano teacher, Aziza Miller

blessed to have a student like her, because then it was not a job. It was fun. And when she started writing on her own, she opened up to me because I had opened up to her about songs that I'd written. I had a friend who had a recording studio, and after school I would take Alicia and another student there and record them. I still have those recordings on cassette.

Alicia graduated early from PPAS, at sixteen, and within a year she had her first recording contract. Both are extraordinary accomplishments, but when it came time to craft *Hell's Kitchen*, Alicia was determined to capture the magical moments of self-discovery that came before she achieved either one.

FIRST STEPS: FINDING A COLLABORATOR

Alicia is no stranger to exploring new artistic pathways: Her creative practice has expanded over the years to include poetry, acting, and fashion design. For *Hell's Kitchen*, she sought a collaborator with expertise in theater, someone who could help deliver not only the emotional beats of this girl's world, but also the specificity of what it meant to grow up in 1990s Hell's Kitchen.

Alicia Keys
This show had to be built in increments, and I went for the book writer first. I interviewed writers before I interviewed directors, before I had any other thoughts.

Alicia teaching the music to the cast during a 2019 reading

There had to be a certain connection to the city. You can't write about a place you don't truly know. For example, I wanted bucket drummers in the show, and that's 1000% a New York experience. Unless you grew up on the trains and on the streets, you are not going to understand the bucket drummers. You had to live it and breathe it and know it. I met a few different people, all great writers. I read a bunch of their work.

In 2010, Kristoffer Diaz's play *The Elaborate Entrance of Chad Deity* was a Pulitzer Prize finalist and was about to be staged for a fourth time, in Los Angeles, at the Geffen Playhouse. Reviewers praised the work for its wickedly intelligent humor as well as its critique of capitalism's need to commodify everything, including identity.

Kris Diaz, book writer

I got an email from my agent in May of 2011. Normally, when they got requests, they would ask me, "Have you ever heard of this organization, and would you like to meet with them?" Instead, they said, "We're setting up a meeting for you with Alicia Keys." My response was, "Yes, yes, you are."

Our meeting was in the wine cellar of her apartment building, and it was super intimidating. But only for a minute, because then we started talking about hip-hop that we liked. Then she told me her idea. She wanted to do a project set in her childhood when she was at Manhattan Plaza.

The meeting seemed to go well, but nothing was decided. A couple of weeks later, I got another message inviting me and my wife, Joanne, to see Alicia perform at the Beacon Theater. It was an intimate show, her and a piano. We were supposed to hang out and meet Alicia afterward, and even though Joanne wasn't feeling well—we didn't know it at the time, but she was pregnant—she said, "I think we should stay." We met Alicia after the show, and we hugged, our families bonded, and that was the beginning of the next thirteen years.

Alicia Keys

When I met Kris, there was no question from the instant we sat down. It was magic, it was electric. I was squealing, I was yelling, I was screaming, "Yo, you remember this," and "Yo, how about this?" We were talking about Mobb Deep and Wu-Tang and Dyckman Houses and Spanish Harlem. You either have traveled those streets or not. That time and place is an unspoken language. You can't teach it, you can't explain it, you can't guide it. Kris was right there with me every step

Kristoffer Diaz, who worked with Alicia to develop the script for *Hell's Kitchen*

"WE KNEW IT WAS A COMING-OF-AGE STORY, BUT WHAT DID THAT MEAN?"

of the way. It was his experience. It was my experience. It was New York's experience. It was our story.

Kris Diaz
It was a fairly conscious decision not to go into that first meeting and say, "This is how we're going to make this musical." The point was to get to know her and for her to know that I understood her language. I understood her musical references. I understood her New York City references. I knew what it was to be growing up in this time. I'm a little bit older than her, and I grew up outside the city, but my family is from the Bronx. I knew where she came from. Then our conversations turned to what we wanted to get across. We knew we needed a story. We needed a traditional beginning, middle, and end. Alicia always knew where she wanted to end. She said, "This can't go any further than the character standing behind the curtain, waiting for her first public performance." She said, "I'm not interested in doing *How I Got Famous*."

The next couple of years were me, Alicia, and Susan Lewis, who at that point was overseeing creative development and production for AKW. We would get in a room together and strategize. Sometimes it would be at Alicia's house, sometimes it would be in her studio—which was pretty relaxing, until you looked over and saw the trophy case with fifteen Grammys in it. I asked a ton of questions. A lot of the work we did was figuring out what the guts of the story were going to be, what the arc was going to look like. We knew it was a coming-of-age story, but what did that mean?

Alicia Keys
How does this girl feel? What is she looking for? Who are the main characters? Why should they be there, what is it about them, and how are they like people who exist in the world? It was *really* fun. I had never done therapy before, and it felt therapeutic to communicate with somebody who had a similar experience to me, but not. Obviously, he's a man, I'm a woman. He's of Hispanic heritage, I'm of Black and white heritage. We had these different perspectives to pull from, but they all made up the diversity and uniqueness of the city. We knew so much about each other's experiences that, in a way, we became best friends. There were phone calls: "What about this?" "I was thinking of..." "I remembered this." We'd spend hours talking and thinking and imagining and dreaming.

Kris Diaz
The character of Miss Liza Jane, Ali's mentor, started when we were talking about Alicia's musical influences. I walked away from that conversation knowing that we had to get them into the show, and that we needed to build a teacher. Once we started to do that, it was easy to figure out who the archetypes were going to be.

Alicia Keys
When Ali meets Miss Liza Jane, it's like when I met Miss Aziza, but it's also what I felt when I first saw Nina Simone perform. That stopped me in my tracks and made me realize there was something inside of me that hadn't awoken yet. Combining people was a fiction, but the barometer we were looking to was emotional truth.

Kris Diaz
After several years of talking and writing, we reached the limits of what we could do on our own. We had been up front with each other from the beginning that neither one of us had ever done this. I had never written a musical from beginning to end. I had worked on musicals, I'd written plays, but I had never had a play produced on Broadway. Now we had a first draft and a treatment and a good sense of what the show was going to be. We didn't know how to take it any further, so we decided to meet with some directors.

MICHAEL GREIF COMES ON BOARD

In 2015, Alicia and Kris interviewed directors, including the widely lauded Michael Greif. Michael, another native New Yorker, has an extensive directorial portfolio, including such shows as *RENT*, *Next to Normal*, and *Dear Evan Hansen*, which earned him a reputation for genre-expanding projects and for rendering nuanced, complex family dynamics.

Michael Greif, director
I was invited to have a meeting with Kris and Alicia. I was already a fan of Kris's work, and we knew each other a bit. Of course, I knew Alicia's music. I was sent

WHO IS MISS LIZA JANE?

The demanding and deeply spiritual Miss Liza Jane character is inspired by multiple women who provided mentorship and guidance to Alicia along the way. Her paternal grandmother, Vergil DiSalvatore, lived in nearby Uniondale, Long Island, and was a regular presence in Alicia's childhood, modeling compassion, elegance, and how to look people in the eye. Alicia's first piano teacher, fellow Manhattan Plaza resident Margaret Pine, helped her establish a strong technical foundation. Singer-songwriter, pianist, and civil rights activist Nina Simone affected Alicia musically and politically: Alicia wholeheartedly absorbed Simone's belief that "an artist's job is to reflect the times." And Alicia's high school music teacher, Aziza Miller, showed Alicia a living, breathing example of the musician she could become.

NINA SIMONE

Margaret Pine

Vergil DiSalvatore

Aziza Miller

a treatment beforehand because, as I remember it, the meeting was a kind of interview to see how I felt about the material and how I might contribute to it.

While all the relationships they'd introduced were of vital importance, I was really pleased to read that the work was an examination of the main character's early years, and not a piece about how Alicia became a recording artist. I do believe that musicals work best when they're most universal. And while everyone can *admire* someone's ascent to pop stardom, the trials and mistakes that every kid makes seemed like a wonderful, universal story that everybody could hook into. Of course, you're dealing with a rather remarkable kid here. There was also a wit, a cleverness, a bravery, and a courage—and also a delusionary aspect—to this kid that were really appealing.

I imagine *Dear Evan Hansen* was in the air, because it had opened on Broadway the previous year. I thought, *Maybe I'm the new guy who you talk to about adolescent musicals*. I later found out that Alicia saw *RENT* as a kid and really liked it, and Kris has always been an unabashed fan of that show.

Kris Diaz

I owe so much of what I do as an artist to Michael, even if it weren't for this project. I saw *RENT* at New York Theatre Workshop when I was seventeen or eighteen years old. I sat in the front row. Taye Diggs spat on me. Idina Menzel mooned me a foot away from my face. They sang "Seasons of Love" right on top of me. I wasn't quite living the life of those people dancing on the table at the Life Cafe, but I was doing similar stuff. I understood community. I understood that in art, we get together to make a thing, and that's all we can really do in the face of life. Michael was already one of the most influential artists in my life because of *RENT*. Yes, it's Jonathan Larson's show, but Michael crafted it. Michael carried it.

Michael's reaction to our treatment was, "You've done something really smart here. You've written a love story between a mother and a daughter." He said, "That's smart artistically, and that's smart from a business perspective, because mothers and daughters come to the Broadway theater." That was the moment when Alicia and I looked at each other and knew. We'd found the right person.

The character of Ali's mother, Jersey, had been a central component since we started. But we didn't know that the weight of that mother-daughter story was so strong that it needed to be our main connective tissue. Once Michael helped us figure that out, then everything that we had already been working on slotted into place. Start with the mom, end with the mom. Everything else fits inside that container.

Michael Greif and Alicia at a rehearsal at the Public Theater

Michael left that first meeting feeling in sync with how Kris and Alicia thought about the piece, and excited about the freshness of this love story between a girl and a single mom who sacrificed her own dreams to build dreams for her child. The trio got to work.

Michael Greif

There were still a lot of variables to decide in terms of which songs were in, which songs weren't in. Every relationship would change and morph considerably, but what was already there was the remarkable bones of the story. Alicia's book, *More Myself*, had not been published at the time, but during the COVID pandemic I got to read it, and I saw how much these formative years were on her mind. The book helped inform what aspects of the story we should elucidate most in the musical.

Much of our work was balancing acts. From the beginning, we all agreed that the mother-daughter relationship would be the longest arc in the musical. It would be what everything else hung on. There was always a very important mentor figure in the apartment complex, but that character and her songs changed almost completely. There was always a dad who behaved similarly to the dad we now have. And there was always a love interest. We tried out a lot

"THE WEIGHT OF THAT MOTHER-DAUGHTER STORY WAS SO STRONG THAT IT NEEDED TO BE OUR MAIN CONNECTIVE TISSUE."

of different potential love songs; considering the size of Alicia's catalog, you had your choice. The balance of where the love interest and the teacher fit in was evolving all the time.

We were all committed to there being a great tragedy in Ali's life, and there were different versions of what that tragedy was before we landed on making the teacher sick. She and Ali would have a very, very meaningful, but very, very short experience together.

Alicia at an early reading of *Hell's Kitchen* in 2019

Alicia Keys

The same way I felt about Kris was how we felt when we met Michael. It was instant. Kris and I were the dreamers, and we were extra creative and wanting to push all the boundaries and do things that hadn't been done and bring fresh energy and not be the same old same old. Then Michael came in, and he had structure and wisdom.

Kris and I had this no limit/no boundaries mentality, and Michael would say, "Here is what musical theater is. This has to happen, and then this has to happen, and then we have to go here, and then we have to go there. And that's how it works." We for sure challenged that in a lot of ways. I didn't care what was usually done; we were going to do it differently. But Michael's understanding of how to tell the story in a way that was going to give you the necessary beats was exactly what we needed. It was a beautiful marriage of new perspective and experimentation with someone who was firmly planted in this space. We couldn't have asked for anything better.

Michael is known among colleagues for his candor, but also for his willingness to experiment and collaborate on every aspect of a show, from character development to lighting design.

Alicia Keys

Michael is definitely straight, no chaser, and we love that. Catch Michael when he's feeling kind of stressed, and he can be sharp. He's not here to play around, and that's what we needed. We needed to get it done. So that's his energy, but really, he's the sweetest, kindest, smartest, wisest, most curious person. He's not demanding, but his suggestions make you think, *Oh, maybe I'm wrong*. How many times I was wrong with him! I would say, "I'm not doing that. That's not right." He'd say, "Just try it. Let's see." I'd say, "Alright, I'll try it, but I don't like it." And then we would try it, and I would look at him. "Damn, you're right. It's better."

According to Kris, one of Michael's great gifts is time management: making the best use of everyone's energies and planning for what's next. In 2017, Michael instigated the first small reading of the script-in-progress. With a skeleton troupe of performers in rented studio space at the edge of the theater district, they began to embody the words on the page.

Alicia Keys

We had to get a sense of what this was feeling like. What was it looking like? How does it work? We had

Alicia, the cast of *Hell's Kitchen*, and Manhattan Plaza residents on the set of the "Kaleidoscope" music video, filmed at Manhattan Plaza

"SHE STARTED TALKING, AND WE HIT IT OFF. WE DECIDED TO MAKE A MUSICAL TOGETHER."

been doing that in our own universes, going away and writing and thinking and then coming back together. We had spent a lot of hours in my studio, the three of us brainstorming and chopping it up and listening to music. Over the years, as we were writing this, I was also making more music, so I would share the latest thing I was working on and we'd ask each other, "What are we missing? What are we needing?"

Kris Diaz
Finally, because he's the one who always pushes things forward, Michael said, "It's enough. We did this. This is great, but to level up we need to get another partner. We need to figure out who's going to really engage in this with us."

GOING PUBLIC

Kris Diaz
At some point very early on, Michael had said, "When you guys feel ready, we'll go to Oskar Eustis [the artistic director of the Public Theater], and we'll tell him that he can do the show." It wasn't, "Do you want to do the show?" We could make the offer, and that was a fun position to be in.

Mandy Hackett, co-producer
Back in 2015, I heard Alicia might be working on a musical. Then I found out that Michael Greif was working with her on it. Years before I worked at the Public, I worked as the literary manager at New York Theatre Workshop when Michael did the world premiere of *RENT* there. We had since done several shows together at the Public, and so I called up Michael. I said, "I hear that there's an Alicia Keys musical. You have to show this to us." And he said, "We're not ready." Every couple of months I would ping him and say, "How's the Alicia Keys musical? I really want to see it. Don't worry if it's not finished. We like to see stuff in the beginning stages." And he would say, "It's not ready."

Finally, after a year had passed, I spoke to Michael, and said, "How's the musical coming?" He said, "Actually, I think we have something we're ready

The exterior of the Public Theater in New York City

to share with you." Oh my God, I was so excited. So they sent the script that they had been working on and came in and met with me and Oskar Eustis at the Public. Honestly, I will never forget the day that Alicia walked into the office. Sometimes meeting people you look up to and respect can be disappointing, because they're not always what you hope them to be. Alicia was what I hoped and so much more. She was so smart, thoughtful, poised, self-possessed. I remember we're sitting around in Oskar's office, and everyone was talking, and she was listening. At a certain point in the meeting, I noticed Alicia hadn't said anything. I finally said, "Well, what do you think, Alicia?" She started talking, and we hit it off. We decided to make a musical together.

Michael Greif, Alicia, and Kris Diaz at the *Hell's Kitchen* premiere at the Public Theater

TERRIA JOSEPH'S BALANCING ACTS

After Terria Joseph graduated from New York University's theater department, she plunged into the city's performing arts scene. She made her mark early on in the 1969 La MaMa production of Ed Bullins's play *It Has No Choice*, and went on to work with many theater companies.

Unlike the character of Jersey, the mother in *Hell's Kitchen* who gives up acting entirely, Terria juggled motherhood, work, and performing. When Alicia was still a baby, Terria took on a role that is still one of her most cherished: In 1981, she played opposite Antonio Fargas in a production of *Dutchman*, written by LeRoi Jones (later known as Amiri Baraka).

"I never stopped," Terria says. "I tried to do stuff at night, and because I already spent enough time away from Alicia, I would bring her to my rehearsals. I was working down at the Henry Street Settlement and the Public Theater, and they didn't mind. She might fall asleep in the audience, or she might cry if my character was getting beat up, but mostly she was quiet. She was shyer than shy back then. I didn't do all that much when she was a kid, but I always tried to be available if opportunities came along, because I was hanging onto the hope of hopes that it wouldn't always be this way."

Alicia remembers that when she was growing up, theater was a way for her and her mother to connect. "It created some of my core memories," she says, "including standing on the TKTS line where we would get half-price tickets to see Broadway shows. Her world and her artistry really poured a lot into me as a young creative person. I discovered all these different ways of expression."

Once Alicia reached adulthood, Terria turned her focus back to performing. Her list of roles over the past few decades is long and varied, including

Antonio Fargas and Terria Joseph in *Dutchman*

theater, television, film, and Alicia's "Like You'll Never See Me Again" music video, in which she plays an ER doctor. For her seventieth birthday, Terria wrote and performed a one-woman show called *Going Through Life with No Direction*.

Once *Hell's Kitchen* signed on with the Public Theater, Alicia asked her mother to join the project as a co-producer. "You can't just decide to enter the Broadway universe," Alicia says. "There's a respect and a history that have to be there for there to be credibility. Because my mother is such a heavy theater actor and is so respected in the theater world, it gave me another level of legitimacy. So many of the experienced artists we encountered along the way would say, 'I was in this piece with your mother,' or, 'I know your mom from this.' It was beautiful to see the Broadway community connect with her and give her her flowers. That's part of the reason why *Hell's Kitchen* is so meaningful to me, because sometimes these dreams become deferred, and you don't exactly know how they're going to come back around, or if they ever will."

"HER WORLD AND HER ARTISTRY REALLY POURED A LOT INTO ME AS A YOUNG CREATIVE PERSON."

Alicia and Terria

Alicia and Terria together during *Hell's Kitchen* rehearsals

2

CHOSEN FAMILY

This page: Maleah Joi Moon (Ali) backstage

Previous page: Shoshana Bean (Jersey) and Maleah Joi Moon (Ali) embracing on opening night of *Hell's Kitchen* on Broadway

THE PUBLIC LIFE

Hell's Kitchen's associate director, Monet, says that making a musical is like building a giant ship. It takes a tremendous collective effort over many years to combine many complex parts. "This is a challenging medium," Monet says, "but if you get all the right pieces together, you can make magic." Alicia Keys, Kris Diaz, and Michael Greif had already put years into the project when they joined forces with the Public Theater in the spring of 2018.

Once at the Public, construction of the "giant ship" escalated, and despite the COVID pandemic, readings and workshops carried on—whether in person or on computer screens.

Michael Greif, director

In the earliest readings, there were a lot of events in the script that I didn't imagine would remain in the play, but we were giving them a little outing. There was a really wonderful sense of, *Let's just see what it feels like to have a leading character who has so much narration*. Everyone involved in the process, even at that point, was remarkably supportive and openhearted.

At the same time, key decisions were being made about the scope of the production, the direction of the story, and how to flesh out the cast.

Alicia Keys

Working with the Public was 1000% an incredible experience. We were now surrounded by other creative minds whose business it was to craft these pieces. They were respectful of the form and of us as artists, wanting to make sure they didn't impose, but prompting and pushing and asking the questions: *What does this mean? What are we saying here?* You can get caught up in what you know, and then you get perspective from folks outside of it, and it gives you clarity.

Oskar Eustis, artistic director, Public Theater

We have all experienced Alicia's artistry, but I felt like I was seeing a glimpse of its foundation: a woman who has always refused to settle for anything but the best. It was also her humility about not pretending she knows what she doesn't know. She knew what she thought, and she would say it, but she'd listen to everybody else. For some people, having power means you surround yourself with sycophants who never disagree with you. Opposite with Alicia. She's using

Rehearsal for an early reading of *Hell's Kitchen*

THE PUBLIC THEATER
PUTTING ART FIRST

"THEATERGOERS ACTUALLY WANT THINGS THAT HAVE INTEGRITY."

New York's Public Theater is one of the earliest nonprofit theaters in the country, founded in 1954 by Joseph Papp. Papp began with the series Shakespeare in the Park, and in 1967 expanded the Public's mission to include new work, establishing its East Village headquarters in the former Astor Library. The first play Papp staged there was the world premiere of *Hair*.

"Here's why it was a good idea that *Hell's Kitchen* came to the Public," says artistic director Oskar Eustis, who has led the Public since 2005. "There is this huge advantage in developing a show that has so much commercial pressure on it in an environment where the institution is not thinking about that. The whole institution is geared toward the idea that we want this show to be the best possible version of itself. Everybody in this organization is trained that way, thinks that way, and believes that. As it happens, doing that often leads to spectacular commercial success, but not because you're aiming at commercial success. It's because theatergoers actually want things that have integrity, that are real, and that are not made out of focus groups trying to guess what an audience is going to like. That is death to creativity.

"Everything from *Hair* to *A Chorus Line* to *Hamilton* to *Fun Home* to *Hell's Kitchen* has prospered because it's grown up in a place that really just asks the question, 'What does this show want to be?' If it's going to have a big commercial life, great. And if it's not, that's also fine. We've made it what it is, and that's the value proposition we use in developing shows."

Program cover pages from Off-Broadway productions of *Hamilton* (2015), *Fun Home* (2013), and *A Chorus Line* (1975)

The Public Theater's façade

her power to make sure she's surrounded by people who are the best at what they do, who will challenge her, support her, lift her up to be the best.

Alicia Keys
Hell's Kitchen has been, for sure, the best project I've ever worked on. I think it's because it was such a long process. It gave me time to understand more about who I am as a human, as a woman, as an artist, and also to have arrived in a place where I don't feel threatened by other amazing, wonderful people. When I first started out in music, I wanted so badly to show people that I had what it took, that I almost boxed people out. It was so important to me that they know: I can contain this, I can hold this. By the time I got around to this project, all that stuff had floated away. I could just be who I am, knowing that collaboration can make the most beautiful things.

Oskar Eustis
Alicia was more involved than the vast majority of theater composers. About three months before we went into rehearsal, she asked to have a meeting so we could go through the set budget. This has never happened to me in my fifty years as an artistic director. It was over budget, and I was in the process of bashing heads and getting it down. We went through line by line, and by the time we were done, she had cut $300,000. And guess what? When she told everybody about those cuts, not a peep. Everybody just nodded. She was so involved in the detail, so committed to it, and so determined that the show had to be the best it could possibly be.

CASTING A WORLD

Two aspects of world-building on everyone's minds at all times were place and race. Because so many members of the show's creative team—starting with Alicia Keys, Kris Diaz, and Michael Greif—are either native New Yorkers or have lived there for decades, the city would have to be depicted in an authentic, textured way, with a reality that transcended tourist tropes.

Oskar Eustis
The writer Bernard Malamud said once that all art has to have an address, meaning it has to come from someplace specific. And we know the building this show came from. We know the floor of the building this show came from.

Kris Diaz, book writer
I get asked a bunch of times, "How did you write this? You're not a seventeen-year-old girl." I say, "I'm also not Black, I'm also not white. I'm Puerto Rican from New York City." My kids are half Puerto Rican, half Filipino, and they have, on more than one occasion, said we don't really do anything specific to our

Maleah Joi Moon (Ali) at a 2024 rehearsal

Chris Lee (Knuck) and Maleah Joi Moon (Ali) at a 2023 rehearsal

ethnicities. I say, "Your heritage is New York City as much as it is anything else." Part of that cultural heritage is difference.

Alicia's experience of growing up in a multilaterally diverse community was largely positive, but she didn't want to present a sugarcoated version of that world. At the same time, she didn't want to sensationalize its inherent conflicts. She and her collaborators worked to organically incorporate a distinctly New York tapestry of identities into the story. They aimed to honestly represent America's complex racial landscape without exploiting it for dramatic impact.

Monet, associate director
Every scene in this play deals with race in some way, shape, or form. It is a part of the conversation almost all the time. We would have done a disservice to the play if we weren't enriching the beats with those feelings.

Oskar Eustis
There was a draft of the script where Knuck, Ali's love interest, was shot by the police. It was very powerful. God knows, police shooting young Black men for no reason is real. But the creative team consistently leaned against artificially raising the stakes or anything melodramatic that took the primary focus off the mother/daughter relationship. I'm so happy with where they ended up. You get what you need to get about how the world treats a young Black man making music on the streets. You absolutely understand that racism is surrounding him and affecting his life choices, but you get that without him having to be killed and becoming a national headline... Knuck's brush with the police is what happens to every young Black man. This is the water they swim in. This is the air they breathe. And isn't that a way more important story to understand?

Michael Greif
I was always intrigued by the notion of what it meant to Ali to be a mixed kid. What were the challenges, what were the joys? But Alicia cautioned us to be subtle in our treatment of racial identity and interactions. For example, there was always a tremendous amount of affection between Ali and Jersey, even in their fury, so we were careful about the times in which Ali accuses Jersey of being a dumb white woman. They're judiciously chosen, and they're specifically about Knuck's safety. Ali does say right at the top, "Can you believe who my mother is?" It's not only that Jersey's brash and aggressive, it's that she's white.

Brandon Victor Dixon (Davis) and Shoshana Bean (Jersey) performing "Fallin'"

Monet
I think a big reason why Michael was interested in having me around was because I could navigate that stuff with him from a different vantage point.

Michael Greif
This is a story about a young Black woman, so the smartest possible thing I could do was to make room for other really smart Black women. The opportunity for me to have a Black associate director was key.

Monet
When we were building the show, we talked about what it meant for a white mother to be raising a little Black girl. While it is not always articulated, it is always present. It would be a different show if Jersey was talking the whole time about being a white mom. Our play is about a mother and a daughter, not a white mother and a Black daughter. However, all those things are present all the time.

This was the '90s, so it was a different time for interracial couples. Jersey likely walked around knowing that there were Black women who felt a type of way about her raising this young Black woman, and while she is strong and confident, that doesn't mean she isn't a little insecure about that. At the time her daughter is railing against her, as they do at that age, the woman that Ali has latched onto is a Black woman. But when Jersey comes to see Miss Liza Jane, do they talk about it? No. Is it in that entire scene? 100%.

Michael Greif
Jersey is particularly threatened by Liza Jane because she can give Ali things that Jersey feels she can't. That is among the things that are making Jersey feel so desperate, and the key to this scene is her desperation. I actually find Jersey quite understandable and likable, even when she's rude. Jersey's not used to asking people for help. She's really bad at it. I love scenes in which people are trying to do things in the worst possible way, but from the greatest emotional need.

Monet
What Michael does that is so especially extraordinary is how he enriches characters and makes them full and dimensional. He does that by understanding who these people are in their entirety, not just who they are in the parts of the play that we see.

Once the show came to the Public, responsibility for matching actors to roles fell to casting directors

> "This should not be a cast of just one thing. It should feel like Manhattan Plaza. It should feel multi-generational. It should feel like New York."

Heidi Griffiths and Kate Murray. For them, the project presented a unique opportunity to hold a mirror up to a world they experience every day.

Kate Murray, casting director
Alicia told us that, always and in every way, this should not be a cast of just one thing. It should feel like Manhattan Plaza. It should feel multi-generational. It should feel like New York.

Heidi Griffiths, casting director
That was the most extraordinary directive for us to have as New York casting directors. *Oh, you mean we can actually create a world on stage that is the world we see every morning when we leave our homes?* It doesn't get better. I don't think you see this kind of diversity in many other musicals. I really don't.

DAVIS

On the one hand, Davis, Ali's father, is playful and openhearted; on the other, he's completely unreliable. Michael Greif needed an actor who could walk that fine line, and he immediately thought of Brandon Victor Dixon.

Michael Greif
Brandon is a great interpreter of pop music. He can really imbue lyrics in pop songs with meaning. I knew that about him. I also knew him as a really clever actor who digs into what the playwright says about the character and tries to find a way to both fulfill that and surprise us all.

Brandon Victor Dixon, actor (Davis)
The key to Davis is that he has his limitations, and he's very open and honest about those. He expects others to accept those things, but he understands if they have challenges doing so.

Michael Greif
Brandon's Davis is unbelievably likable. It's sort of superhuman, what he gets away with. Brandon's the only actor on that stage who was there from the very beginning, and the first person about whom Alicia said, "Oh, let's keep him. He should do this."

Alicia Keys
Davis is this complex person who is simultaneously loved and hated. He says and does things that make you think, *Come on, man, why would you do that?* At the same time, you see why he's so attractive to people.

Brandon Victor Dixon

We had to have that complexity, and we had to have this incredible voice that could sing songs that a woman normally sings. There had to be a tenderness but also playfulness and the ability to explore the voice in a way that was unusual.

Michael Greif

Davis reflects the sophistication of Alicia's thinking and Kris's writing, not shying away from the complexities of expectations and failed expectations. And there are other Black men in this show who are really upright and who do all the right things, so we don't have the burden, luckily, of only having one Black guy on the stage.

Kris Diaz

We had a big meeting after one of the workshops. Members of Alicia's team were there, including her husband, Swizz Beatz. I remember looking at Swizz while I was talking to the group. I said, "I'm not writing a *Black Men Ain't Shit* show." At the same time, the reality of the character Alicia described had to be negligent toward his child. That was tricky for us. People hated Davis at the Public and they hate him on Broadway. They love Brandon, they love the songs, but they take it out on him. When Davis doesn't show up for dinner, it's heartbreak. You hear Ali as she watches the clock, saying "It's 6:00 and 6:30, and..." and there are people in the audience who get it instantly. Before she finishes saying "6:30" you hear pockets in the audience saying, "That motherfucker. He did it again."

To balance that, we needed to figure out his redeeming qualities. We had to make that guy be a passionate artist with a lust for life. The reason his name is Davis is that Alicia and I watched Sammy Davis Jr. perform "Mr. Bojangles" in the tightest pants you've ever seen in your life. And we both sat there and agreed, *This little dude is everything*. You get why people would be hypnotized and seduced by him. This guy could do the smallest gestures and soft-shoe and it wasn't just about performing, it was getting at something deep inside. Brandon got it instantly. *And* he sings.

Heidi Griffiths

Some of the decisions Davis makes are deeply problematic, and yet you cannot have the audience shut down to him. He sings some of the most iconic Alicia Keys songs in the show, and you need people to be excited when he starts. Having a beautiful voice is helpful, of course, but perhaps even more helpful is having that openness and warmth that Brandon brings, so he can play a flawed man who has incredibly good intentions, but not the ability to follow through on them.

Monet

Davis is the hardest track to direct because of the nuance required. Davis is who he is, and it is our expectations of what we want him to be that he can't fulfill, because that's not who he is. There's no malice in him. He's a great example of the full characters that Michael creates through his direction. He could have made Davis slimy and gross, but he's charming and fantastic. And that's why you wish that he wanted to be this other thing. The humanity Brandon brings to that character is incredible.

TINY

When Ali isn't puppy-dogging after Knuck or going at it with her mother, she's hanging out with her two homegirls, Tiny and Jessica. In their full teenage glory, the three are consistently down for adventure, committed to being current on all the trends, and, for the most part, unbreakably bonded. Tiny is that friend who has an ounce more maturity than the others; she operates from the position "You better check yourself before you wreck yourself." When Alicia coached on the television show *The Voice* in 2017, singer Vanessa Ferguson—originally from Brooklyn—joined her team, which led to an unexpected casting opportunity.

Vanessa Ferguson on opening night for *Hell's Kitchen* on Broadway

Vanessa Ferguson (Tiny) performing "Girl on Fire"

Alicia Keys
As soon as I met Vanessa, she was ridiculously special to me. I loved her style. I loved the way she wore her hats. I loved her hair and the clothes she chose. She had this husky, super beautiful voice that was reflective of Roberta Flack and Dionne Warwick. There's so much life and experience in it. She wowed me every time, and when I found out that she could rhyme, I thought, *Oh my gosh, I love this girl. She has it all.*

***The Voice* asks audiences to vote on contestants after each performance round, winnowing the field until one ends up victorious. Vanessa ended up in a tie for fifth place.**

Vanessa Ferguson, actor (Tiny)
When we realized I wasn't moving on and Alicia came up onstage to hug me, she said, "Leave your number with my people."

Alicia Keys
I always knew exactly what Tiny was supposed to look and sound and feel like. I realized Vanessa had all that, but I had no idea if she could act. And then when she came in, she was able to embody so much of Tiny's irreverence and "I don't care" attitude. She did it with ease. On top of it, she was able to sing, and she anchored all the harmonies so beautifully.

Vanessa Ferguson
Alicia called about six months after *The Voice* ended to say, "I have this project I think you'll be perfect for." I've always been interested in acting but never had the opportunity to see if I even liked it. They flew me up from North Carolina for a reading in the town where I was born and raised. I loved it. I wanted more of it.

Kate Murray
Vanessa has this gorgeous sound, and she is just an effortless actor. Even in early readings, she always got every laugh. She has such great instincts. She was such an indispensable part of the project that whenever we heard from producing that we were going to do another reading, we'd say, "Just make sure Vanessa's travel is budgeted for."

Vanessa Ferguson
Tiny is very chill, very sure of herself and where she fits in the world. She has her own opinions and is a little stubborn. I try to make sure that Tiny has fun and smiles, because I don't think she's a total cynic. She's just a realist. She's afraid of Ali's mom, and she's afraid of major consequences. I think she realizes that the girls are at a time in their lives where they have more freedom, but their frontal lobes haven't developed all the way, and their choices can really affect their futures. She's the mother of the gang, trying to make sure everybody stays in line and isn't doing anything too crazy while they're out in the streets.

When she was on *The Voice*, Vanessa wrote a rap for the beginning of a Rihanna song, but when she brought it to a rehearsal, the musical director told her that original lyrics weren't allowed. Alicia asked to hear it anyway, so Vanessa performed it and then thought that was the end of that.

Alicia Keys
When we got to "Girl on Fire," we wanted Vanessa to write the rhyme, because she's a writer and an artist already. It was perfect.

Michael Greif
The song "Girl on Fire" essentially says, *Wow, she's great. Wow, she's great*. And we knew, in the context of this story, that we needed to make sure there were dissenting opinions about how great it was all going. Tiny seemed like the person for that, and the rap was going to be a good way of getting additional information in. We wanted there to be something that undercut the huge enthusiasm of the song, and pretty early on, we recognized that we could have Ali's friend dogging her a little.

Vanessa Ferguson
While I'm onstage doing the rap, I'm able to look around and reflect not just on how I've come such a long way, but on the fact that where I'm from, there was no hope or promises given to me outside of what I

had in my own head. I'm aware of how rapping is not a traditional Broadway thing, so we're doing something that's out of the box, but also how special it is that Alicia would trust me and see the value in me to be the person to do that. Because I rap with a handheld microphone, it almost feels like I'm stepping back into my own world, where I just have a mic and it's me and the stage. It's only sixteen bars, but I have this huge moment to be myself.

KNUCK

Once the creative team centered the story on Ali's relationship with Jersey, Knuck's character was scaled back, but he remains critical to Ali's development as a young woman. In particular, his experiences push her to see beyond her adolescent self-interest. Knuck has to be appealing but not slick, and he has to live on the tightrope between how society sees him and who he actually is.

Kate Murray
Heidi and I were casting a version of Disney's *Hercules* as part of our Public Works initiative, and Chris Lee was submitted by his agent for the title role. With his arms, we thought, he'll be perfect. He came in, and it wasn't quite a fit. The next day, though, we were having auditions for the *Untitled Kris Diaz/Michael Greif Project*. We asked Chris to come in and sing a song of his choice.

Chris Lee

Alicia Keys
Knuck has to come across as a real embodiment of New York energy, and yet he also needs to be charming and unconventionally attractive even as there's a roughness about him. There's a strength and weight there. But when you take off the mask, as we see him do in "Gramercy Park," you find someone who's also vulnerable and beautiful and layered. He has to possess all of this in a limited amount of scenes. Chris is able to naturally have all the character components that are needed, so when he's onstage, you know exactly who you are looking at. It's pure. Also, he has a killer, incredible, unbelievable voice. He loves harmonies. Sometimes you gotta reel Chris back: *Hold on, Chris. Come back. Wait a minute, you've gone too far.* But it's amazing to work with somebody like that, because if you can't have someone go crazy, you don't know where you can go.

Chris Lee, actor (Knuck)
After the *Hercules* audition, Heidi and Kate told my agent I'd be better suited for this other thing, but they couldn't tell us what it was. I had to sign an NDA. I really wanted to do *Hercules*. I wanted to be Black-ass Disney Hercules. I wanted to make some history there. My agent said, "I'm just saying this other thing seems very important, because they have Greif attached." I didn't put together who Michael Greif was until the first reading, when I realized, *Oh, you're the guy from the* RENT *documentaries*. I looked up his resume, and then I understood. *Oh, you're the man*. I get there day one, and looking at the lyrics, I recognized that these were Alicia Keys songs. *What is this?* And then she walks in. I thought, *Get out of here, bro, like, get the hell out of here*.

Kris Diaz
We had to find a way to do the love story without spending a ton of time on it. How could we show that sensitive side of Knuck without signposting it? "Gramercy Park" was a real gift to us, figuring out that we were going to place the song in his mind. It becomes no longer about the girl seeing him. It's about people in the outside world seeing him. That was Knuck opening up to Ali, and that was a real reason for them to fall for each other.

Chris Lee
"Gramercy Park" is such a hard song to sing. It doesn't operate like your typical musical theater song. It doesn't

Chris Lee as Knuck

have this beginning, middle, end. It's just these abstract questions and then this declaration and realization that some people are judging you not based on who you are. It's four stanzas and a chorus. You don't get a lot of time to convince anybody of anything; you just gotta tell the truth.

I remember going into it thinking, *They're gonna hate me. They're gonna think I'm boring*. I consider myself a singer, and so while everyone else gets to do all these crazy runs and scream—and I'm the one who can probably outrun anybody—I didn't get to do none of that. I had to sit there. That discipline was amazing. I love a challenge. And that was a challenge, that restraint, that discipline, that honesty. Because you can ask anybody, I didn't oversing, I didn't overact, I didn't overdo anything. You wouldn't even know my personality from that role, which is what I enjoyed. I really got to be somebody else.

Kate Murray

Like Brandon, Chris brought incredible warmth to the part. Knuck is complicated because you have to feel there's nothing predatory about him, even though he's much older than Ali. Chris had everything: the charm, the sex appeal, the humor, and then that voice.

Michael Greif

Chris was wonderfully helpful to me, especially in the development process. It's hard to stage things like "Unthinkable." You have to create events and you have to create story, and he was so open to investigating what stories could be told.

Chris Lee

What makes Knuck special to me is that everything you think you know when you first see him, you have to rethink. He has to wear a tank top, and you gotta see his drawers, and he gotta be wearing Timbs. He gotta have a gold watch on and some gold chains and some diamond earrings. And to have my dreadlocks on top of it, man, in the '90s this kid would have been a white mother's dream, right? So let's just walk into what people are already thinking, then he opens his mouth. When he does not respond to this girl how she believes he should, we realize we didn't think he was going to sound like that. Knuck is the epitome of not judging a book by its cover.

ALI

The role of Ali would be demanding for the most seasoned actress, but because audiences had to believe she's only seventeen years old, the casting directors had to fill this enormous part with a relatively young performer.

Alicia Keys
I'll tell you what, Ali was not easy to cast. We were looking for a girl who was strong-minded but also could relate to that angst you feel when you're not getting the space to be who you are. We needed an unbelievable singer with the technical proficiency of a superstar recording artist. We needed somebody who could be innocently unaware and oblivious and in the first forays of love and independence. And then we also needed her to be an amazing dancer with a sense of movement that could capture your attention. She had to narrate the entire show as if you were her best friend, and all of that had to come in a package that was close to seventeen. That is insane, like crazy insane.

Kate Murray
We did a massive search for Ali. We saw actors we'd heard of and folks from the music world, and then we opened it up to agents. That's how Maleah came to us.

Because of the timing, Maleah didn't do any of the music, they just did the scenes, and the scenes were captivating. They sent us a TikTok of themself singing "I'd Rather Go Blind" by Etta James. Heidi and I both sat up straight. Because it was TikTok, though, we couldn't tell if it was real.

Heidi Griffiths
It was a real pinch-me moment. We were both thinking, *Are you thinking what I'm thinking? That our work is done now?*

Maleah was at a crossroads when they received the invitation to audition. They'd left college after two years, had moved back home to New Jersey, and were feeling adrift, personally and artistically.

Maleah Joi Moon, actor (Ali)
When *Hell's Kitchen* came onto my radar, I remember thinking, *Are you sure they want me to audition for this? I have no experience*. And my agent, Sheri Talkovsky, said, "Just go and do it." In the days leading up to the audition, I was struggling to learn the material. It was a very fast casting process, so I didn't get to have a coaching session or anything like that.

Maleah Joi Moon

Kate Murray
We had them in for a callback and asked them to sing something they loved, and they sang "Home" from *The Wiz*. When they were able to sing this thing they loved, everything that they would be able to mine in our music was evident.

Maleah Joi Moon
The acting sides, that was my juice. I was very excited about that. I wasn't good on the music. I felt very shaky. The overarching thing, or maybe the subconscious thing, was that I didn't feel worthy of a project attached to the Public. The day before the audition, I called Sheri and said, "I can't do this. I don't want to go in there and embarrass myself." I am so glad that she took the reins and said, "Girl, no. You're gonna go into the room and no matter what happens in there, now the people at the Public and Michael Greif know your name. We're going."

I went in there, and it was the most nerve-wracking experience and, equally, the most fun I have had in an audition room ever. I sang "Home" from *The Wiz*. They asked why I'd sung that, and I said it was because I didn't know the material. I did the monologue, and Michael coached me while we were in the room, and I remember taking the adjustments and feeling like, *Whoa, I'm working right now. I'm nineteen, and I'm working, and this is the craft.*

Alicia Keys

When we first met Maleah, we knew we were discovering someone who was in this unique position of being very organic and untouched. Maleah's very in touch with their emotions, and they were able to deliver all the beats—the parts where you have to be a little gnarly and tough, the parts where you have to be delicate and sensitive, the parts where you have to be fun-loving and fresh. They had all this dynamic and it was unbelievable.

Kris Diaz

I didn't know I was writing this role for Maleah, but I was. I said to them a bunch of times that we wish the show had moved more quickly, but when we started working on the show, they were in fourth grade. So in some ways, the universe had us wait for them, because when they came into the room, we knew pretty quickly that they had something special. They worked really hard in their first audition and then the rest of the way, every time you threw something at them, they were able to take it.

Maleah Joi Moon

I became an Alicia fan at a very young age.

I have a visceral memory of the first day I went in for rehearsal, and Alicia was also there. I remember sitting next to Vanessa Ferguson, and saying, "That's her right there!"

Alicia had just been sitting behind the table, and then she got up while we were learning the music. She would come around and introduce herself with her beautiful speaking voice, and say things like, "How are you today?" and "How are you feeling?" She embraced me from the first day. You would think that, because she's such an international superstar, how does she have time to come and babysit? But she made the time, and we'd have her son Genesis running around the theater while she was teaching music to the understudies. This is the time and the effort that you put in to make sure something stays pure and precious. She checks in with me. I check in with her. She's a stunning human being. I couldn't imagine doing anything like this with anyone other than her.

Shoshana Bean (Jersey) and Maleah Joi Moon (Ali) during rehearsal

Shoshana Bean

JERSEY

Like many single parents, Jersey does what she has to do. In order to raise Ali, she has pushed aside her own artistic ambitions, even though she still lives in a building—and city—full of artists actively pursuing their dreams. She's tough as nails, but we never lose sight of how much she loves her daughter...even when she has trouble communicating that directly.

Alicia Keys
Jersey had to have tough lioness energy and also the vulnerability of a woman who has been protecting her heart and her daughter forever. We needed this complexity, because we were fighting very hard to keep Jersey from becoming witchy. That's not who she is. She's not this complaining, overly aggressive, oppressive woman. Now, she has those tendencies, but it's only because of things we discover as we go along. All of this had to be captured in one of the most powerful vocal performances ever, period, because she had to captivate the audience.

Shoshana Bean, actor (Jersey)
Adam Blackstone (the music supervisor and co-orchestrator for *Hell's Kitchen*) was an acquaintance of mine. We had never worked together, but at some point he presented me to Alicia as an option for this role. They'd gone through a few people and were struggling to find exactly what they wanted. He showed her a video of me singing on Instagram. Then he sent me a screenshot of their conversation where she had responded, "She's it!"

Alicia Keys
Adam sent me this video where Shoshana was casually slaying a song so disrespectfully. I thought, *OMG, what is going on here? We have to see her immediately.*

Shoshana Bean
I got the offer to do a reading, and a couple days in, Alicia pulled me aside and said, "I'd like to ask you to stay with us into the Public production."

Heidi Griffiths
It seemed so obvious that it was Shoshana's role in every regard. There was a magic to what she did to an audience when she began "Pawn It All." It was as if no one in the theater had any will of their own, because Shoshana was orchestrating this unbelievable emotional journey for all of us to go on.

Kate Murray
One of the most difficult things about Jersey is how tough she is. Jersey is a prickly character, and Shoshana fully embraced that. She wasn't afraid of the spikier parts and wasn't afraid of the vulnerability, which is so important, because it underpins everything else. It underpins her connection with every single actress who plays Ali. When they're singing "No One," those tears are real. There was one night where they were afraid the mics weren't going to work because Maleah and Shoshana were crying so much.

Kris Diaz
Shoshana feels so deeply. She is such a "rip open your heart and share it with everybody" kind of person.

Shoshana Bean
I had just played someone's kid the year prior, and so at first this role felt like a really abrupt shift. For women in our business, it meant I'd aged into a different bracket, and I wasn't ready for that. But the gift with this particular show, and this particular mother, is the woman in real life who she is loosely based on.

Being such a fan of Alicia all these years, of course I'd seen footage of her mother, Terri. I'd watched interviews, and I knew Terri came to New York with dreams of being an artist herself. She chose to have a child on her own, and that child ended up being Alicia Keys, who has given the world so much. I was so in awe of someone who would make the sacrifice. I wanted to know, *Who is that woman, and how did she do it?* My dear friend Billy Porter came to see the show and he said, "Shoshana, you're redefining what a mother looks like on the Broadway stage. Ain't never been another mother like this." I tried to make Jersey the sexiest, fieriest, most ferocious, protective, strong mother who sacrificed and scraped and scrapped and did whatever she needed to do.

Jersey's whiteness is largely a side issue in the show, except when she enlists its accorded privilege by calling the cops on three young bucket drummers. It's a perilous lapse that Jersey realizes as soon as Knuck is taken away.

Monet
In developing Jersey, we talked a lot about who Terri was when she was younger. This whole wave we've seen in recent years of everybody trying to be aware and woke and progressive? No, no, no. Coming up, Terri was doing very cool theater with very cool Black people in New York City. But as Michael says, when you have kids, sometimes you make mistakes in your attempt to protect them.

Jersey is very aware of race. Look at her friends in the show. It is in her desperation to take care of her child that she stumbles and makes that mistake. And that moment they have when she's telling Davis about the police is filled with race that we don't talk about explicitly, because she's telling him, "I did this thing." And he knows that she feels awful about it because she knows that it could have gone terribly wrong.

The role's emotional demands are matched—maybe even exceeded—by its vocal challenges.

Alicia Keys
If there is a character who holds the record for the most difficult songs, it would be Jersey, because all of her songs have the highest range. You've got to bring people down and bring them back up, and then you get soft and get crazy loud. Man, you hear and feel Shoshana in this part, and it is literally unforgettable.

Shoshana Bean
When I come into a show, a lot of times the framework is already there. Nothing is being built on me. I felt like Alicia saw what she had with me, and she said, *Let's highlight that without sacrificing the story*. I will always be grateful to her for letting me run and be free.

Alicia and Shoshana Bean at the Shubert Theatre

THE ORIGINAL BROADWAY ENSEMBLE

"THERE WAS ONE WEEK WHERE, OUT OF THE EIGHT SHOWS, I DID FIVE DIFFERENT TRACKS."
—ONYXX NOEL

Michael Greif, director

One of the particular joys of putting a show together is finding the whole community for it. Great care goes into creating the acting ensemble that surrounds the principals. We need to ensure coverage if someone gets sick or has a family emergency; many of the supporting players are also swings and understudies for the larger roles. Their ability to fill those spots is a huge factor in their inclusion. At the same time, you don't want a bunch of similar people onstage. You want to have different flavors and shapes and sizes and ages, and particularly for this story, it's important that there is racial and ethnic diversity. We have been fortunate to populate our ensemble with so much personality and musical ability and spirit.

For her dance ensemble, Camille A. Brown was tasked to find amazing dancers but also find visual diversity within that. She did a spectacular job, which means that you recognize each person, you get who they are from scene to scene to scene. Their individuality is very important to her choreography and to the way Dede Ayite costumed them. You don't get four women or four men who look alike, so you get to know them individually in the course of the evening. You get excited by them in one number, and then you start seeking them in others.

Members of the dance and acting ensembles on opening night

ENSEMBLE, UNDERSTUDIES, SWINGS, AND STANDBYS

Chad Carstarphen
Reid Clarke
Chloe Davis
Nico DeJesus
Timothy L. Edwards
Desmond Sean Ellington
Badia Farha
Vanessa Ferguson
David Guzman
Gianna Harris
Jakeim Hart
Takia Hopson
Jackie Leon
Raechelle Manalo
Jade Milan
Onyxx Noel
Susan Oliveras
Sarah Parker
Aaron Nicholas Patterson
William Roberson
Niki Saludez
Nyseli Vega
Donna Vivino
Lamont Walker II
Rema Webb
Oscar Whitney Jr.

MISS LIZA JANE

Miss Liza Jane is more than a musical mentor and role model for Ali. She is the spiritual center of the Manhattan Plaza community and Ali's guide to her musical, cultural, and racial heritage.

Alicia Keys
We'd been workshopping Miss Liza Jane for so long, trying to figure out how she could be this powerful, exalted queen. You needed gravitas to play Miss Liza Jane. She needed to be like Maya Angelou. She had to have a spirit and energy that was like a quiet storm. And then she had to have this voice that delivered really difficult songs, not only emotionally difficult, but range-wise. And then Kecia Lewis came, and Kecia owned Miss Liza Jane. If you meet Kecia in real life, she's one of the homegirls. When everyone's hanging out and chilling, she's the rawest of them all. But in the role, she transforms.

Kecia Lewis knew Ali and Miss Liza Jane's world firsthand. As a teen, she commuted from Queens into Hell's Kitchen to attend the High School of Performing Arts on West Forty-Sixth Street. Her best friend at school grew up in the same building Alicia would later live in, and Kecia was in and out of it all the time, occasionally sneaking into the Ellington Room, a community space where she and her friends would bang on the piano.

Kecia Lewis

Kecia Lewis, actor (Miss Liza Jane)
I am a dyed-in-the-wool New Yorker, and I believe this show is a love letter to New York and all the eccentrics in it. It's an homage and it's truthful.

Heidi Griffiths
Kecia came into one of the smaller studios across the street from the Public, and we had our camera set up so we could film for Alicia. It was just Kate and me, and we asked her to sing "Perfect Way to Die." She sang the song, and it was absolutely riveting. We were trying to be solicitous and care for her in whatever ways we could, and so afterward we said, "Well, that was amazing. I mean, that was just perfect. But if you're not happy, we have all day. Have as many goes as you want." And she just looked at us and said, "Oh no, you only sing that song once a day."

You can't sit in a theater and hear Kecia sing that song without looking around and seeing all the Black mothers in that space, and how deep the fears and terrors of this world are if you are the mother of a Black boy.

Miss Liza Jane lets Ali know that she has responsibilities—to her musical gifts but also to her community.

Kris Diaz
The thing that's become really clear to me in that character is the role of expectation and rigor. That's what Miss Liza Jane is for this young woman who starts out navel-gazing and very *woe is me*. Miss Liza Jane has the ability to look at someone and say, "Do something about it. You can acknowledge all the hard parts, and that doesn't mean you get to stop fixing them. My expectation of you is that you're gonna do it. So do it."

Kecia Lewis
My goal is to help people recognize that a lot of our mentors are tapped-in spiritually, whatever their spiritual practice or lack thereof. And that's what I want to give onstage. People tell me a lot, they're reminded of a grandma or an auntie who grounded them in a way as a human being, so that when they went out into the world, they were fully themselves.

Michael Greif
That extensive mentorship was always a wonderful part of Liza Jane. And the racial component is so deeply a part of the family dynamic. Liza Jane is Alicia's

Kecia Lewis getting ready to go onstage

PERFECT WAY TO DIE

At the shocking climax of Act One, audiences don't yet know Knuck's fate. We know something bad has happened, but how bad is unclear. Miss Liza Jane sits at the piano and sings the heart-wrenching "Perfect Way to Die," and as she does that, large projections at the back of the stage flash portraits of actual victims of police brutality in America. To do the song and the moment justice, Kecia Lewis had to draw deeply from her artistic reservoir and her own experience as the mother of a Black son.

Kecia Lewis, actor (Miss Liza Jane)
When I met Alicia, she was not what I expected. I came in with my arms folded and a scowl on my face, thinking, *Oh, she's a celebrity. She's going to try to make me sing just like her*. I got the exact opposite. What I got was, "What are you feeling when you sing this? What does it bring up for you? How do you want to sing this?" Even the key I sing in is not the song's original key, and that came from me sitting with the part for a while and recognizing that Miss Liza Jane doesn't sing like everybody else. I started to explore, *How low could I go?* I have four-and-a-half octaves in my range, but I'd never been asked to sing or speak down there. I guess at this age and this role and where I am in my life, it all merged and worked. I asked Alicia and Michael to listen to what I had been working on

for "Perfect Way to Die." Both their mouths fell open, and they said, "Can you do that eight shows a week?" There were times I struggled to reach a couple of notes with full power in my belt, and it would sound rough and scratchy and weird to me. And Alicia said, "It's great. That's what you sound like when you sing. Sometimes it's not perfect."

I look at this song as an important moment I don't ever recall seeing on Broadway, where we are bringing police brutality in the face of the audience in a huge way, without it being watered down or Disneyfied. The work that I have to do before I start the scene, and the work I have to do while I'm singing it, I consider it a privilege. My acting coach, Anthony Abeson, used to say, "Part of your job is to hold the mirror up to nature, and when their mouths are open, either in wonder or laughing, you slip the truth in." That's that moment for me; while people are wondering, *What's happening?* they're going to get that truth. And I consider it a privilege to be able to do that eight shows a week.

My son, Simon, is now twenty-one, but when his dad and I split, he was eight, and I was absolutely terrified. I was very conscious of what having a Black-presenting son would be like, number one in New York City, number two in the culture that we live in. Once he and I were alone, I became hyperconscious of that, because I couldn't be everywhere all the time, and my profession often took me away. I had a whole tribe of people that would help me—other actors and my mom. She has Alzheimer's now, but she would come take care of Simon for me. I tried to only take jobs away from home during summers, when he could go with me.

As Simon became a teenager, I saw the proliferation of new kinds of drugs and a rising suicide rate among teens. And then there's a target on your back because you're a brown boy. When the incident with Trayvon Martin happened—I have a picture of the two of them side by side, they could be brothers.

The way I had to train Simon for how he needed to be in the world broke my heart, but I had to, because I wanted him to come home every day. I joke with Simon sometimes that my knees look like camel knees, as much as I had to pray. I made sure he had a spiritual foundation so that when I wasn't there, or he felt like he was alone even if I was there, he had something higher than me to call on and ask for help. And he got that, and I'm very, very grateful. I'm so proud of him.

When I sing "Perfect Way to Die," all of that is going on.

grandma in a lot of ways. When I read Alicia's book, I recognized the effect that being with her father's mother had in her early life. Liza Jane also became that person. So she's a musical mentor, but she's also a cultural ambassador. She is the link into Ali's Black history that she can't quite get from her dad.

Kecia Lewis
When I was a teenager, I had a moment where I was interested in opera. I was practicing at home, and my dad walked by, and then he came back and said, "Let me ask you something. Do you feel that when you sing it?" I said, "Not really. I think it's more a technical thing that I'm trying to get to, and then I'll get to the feeling part of it." And he said, "If you don't feel it, you don't have a right to sing it." That became a living goal for me. As I got older, it was like, *Yeah, I'm not singing anything that I don't feel*. The voice is the technical part, but the heart and the truth-telling are what people respond to.

JESSICA

Jessica is part of Ali's crew, and in a counterpoint to the self-contained Tiny, she's a spunky, playful free spirit. She's also wary of authority figures, whether that means the police or Ali's mom.

Jackie Leon

Alicia Keys
When Jackie Leon came in the room, when we first interviewed her, she was just insane, like totally insane. She was electric, electrifying—exactly who Jessica is. She just embodied it in every way... Michael loved her from the jump, and so did I.

Kris Diaz
Jessica is the sneaky love bomb in the middle of our play. And Jackie is a love bomb of a human. I don't think there's ever been anybody quite like her on a Broadway stage. We saw some people who had real Broadway experience, but Michael said, "There's something in that one. There's something really particular."

Jackie had recently graduated from the theatre arts program at Marymount Manhattan College and was trying to navigate a barrier-filled industry.

Heidi Griffiths
It's particularly hard on young women who have some form of body diversity, something that does not adhere to societal expectations of what a young woman should look like in a play on Broadway, or a play at the Public Theater, for that matter.

Jackie Leon, actor (Jessica)
It felt like everybody who had this path to Broadway had a certain level of training and dedication that the industry required. I didn't feel like I had that vocal agility. My parents immigrated here from Colombia, and I grew up listening to salsa. I sang a lot of folk. When I started seeing where Black people existed in theater, it was like we had to be exceptionally talented in a way that nobody else is.

My first year at college, there was a voice teacher who was harboring a lot of prejudices against my identity as a Black person. All the music she would get me was in the Black musical theater canon. She would say, "You could play Dorothy in *The Wiz*, but you should really think about what you're wearing. You don't want to look too frumpy." She asked one time if it was okay to say the N-word within the context of a quote. Then I learned musical-theater history and how there was a culture of who was allowed on that stage. For a long time, it wasn't people who looked like me. There were beginning to be shows like *Hamilton* or *In the Heights* or *West Side Story*, and I got excited, and then I thought, *I don't have the body for that*. I started to feel like the specific configuration of my person, someone who sings like me and looks like me, didn't really have a space to exist. I don't want to play

Vanessa Ferguson, Jackie Leon, and Maleah Joi Moon during rehearsal

someone's mother or mammy because of my body type, and I don't want to sing or perform in narratives that are for the white gaze and the white audiences.

Heidi Griffiths
I think Jackie was restless to break through those ceilings that she felt were being put over her because she was short, because she was full of figure, because she was a dark-skinned Latina. As a human being, she has such power, but she didn't quite know it. She has more talent in her little finger than most of the people we auditioned had in their entire beings.

Jackie Leon
It was my second in-person audition ever. I finished the scene, and no one said anything, so I assumed I fucked it up. I said, "I'm so sorry." Michael said, "What?" Then we sang "Girl on Fire," and Michael said, "You did very well here today, Jackie." I was like, *Work*. I left, and I was skipping around on the streets.

Then I get told that they wanted to do a second in-person. Heidi called and said, "Jackie, I want to give you an idea of what to go in with." She gave me a little background of who Jessica was, and how these are the three older girls in the neighborhood. I thanked her for being so nice to me, and she said, with her British accent, "No, Jackie, it's purely selfish, because I feel like this role should be played by someone as talented and as unique as you. Come in and show Alicia who you are."

Kate Murray
When Jackie came in for the callback, we were filming it, and Jackie bounced around with so much energy that the camera couldn't follow. If you look at the tape, the camera is racing to keep up. And then Heidi and I got the incredible privilege that we so rarely get in our job, where we made Jackie the offer to do the workshop. And that workshop was sort of like a wait-and-see: *This is a young actor. We'll see how it goes.*

Jackie Leon
After the workshop I convinced myself that they didn't want me, that I didn't book it. It was imposter syndrome. And then Heidi saw me and said, "We're gonna see you in June for the next workshop. And we'll see you in September, for the Off-Broadway production." At that point, I went up to Alicia. She said, "Yeah, you've just been blowing us away. We love you." And I was like, "Can I hug you, Alicia Keys?" And she was like, "Yeah."

WHO WAS YOUR MENTOR?

OSKAR EUSTIS ON GORDON DAVIDSON

The only person I ever worked for directly was Gordon Davidson, the founder and artistic director of the Mark Taper Forum in Los Angeles. I was thirty, my theater company in San Francisco, the Eureka, was falling apart, and Gordon and I were at a conference together when he offered me a job. He said, "I don't want to interfere with what's going on in your life, but if you were interested in coming to L.A. and working for me, I'd be interested in talking about it." I had never thought of myself as having a career. I was a driven, crazy artist who had companies that made art. I went for a walk with an older friend of mine named Burke Walker, who was the artistic director of a theater in Seattle. I said, "Burke, I don't know how to think about this. I'm a company member." And he said, "Ask yourself where you will be of the most use." That was a huge gift to me, because for the first time, it allowed me to think about my career without being a careerist, which I was allergic to.

I had this unfinished play that was just sprawling out of control, that I'd been working with Tony Kushner on and that I realized the Eureka was not going to be able to do. So I wrote to Gordon and I said, "Dear Gordon, the Berlin Wall has fallen. Communism is dead. My girlfriend left me. My theater company has broken up. My father's dead. I don't know what I believe in anymore, but I believe in this play. If you will agree to produce this play, I will come and work for you." And I sent him the first two acts of *Angels in America*. The next day he called me and said, "Of course I'll produce this play. Come to L.A." And I did. I went and had five years of working for Gordon, and he was immensely influential. My first show on the main stage at the Taper was a failure. It was the biggest show I had ever done, and I was really crushed. Gordon invited a group of eight or nine older directors, many of them famous, to lunch with me. He asked them to go around the table and tell stories of disasters they'd had. I was incredibly moved and impressed by this. What a gift to give me, not to give me notes or a pep talk, but to bring a whole bunch of some of the most successful and powerful people I just idolized, and have them talk about their failures. Gordon had his faults, but boy, what a debt I owe him. I called him "Boss" till the day he died, and I'm just very grateful to have fallen into his care.

TERRIA JOSEPH ON LILLIAN HANHAM DIXON

When I was twelve, I went around my neighborhood in Toledo, Ohio, knocking on doors to get babysitting jobs because I was sick of never having any money. I went to the door of Lillian Hanham Dixon. She had just moved in. She was a dance teacher, and she had two kids. So I babysat, and I took dance classes. She was the one who said, "Okay, you know how to dance. Go to New York and learn how to act." That's a mentor. If that's not a mentor, I don't know what is.

AZIZA MILLER ON PAUL E. WEST

My mentor is ninety-one years old. He's the bass player Paul West. When I was about eighteen, I knew that I wanted to learn how to play jazz. There was a Saturday program for young people called the Jazzmobile Workshop, and it was started by the jazz pianist Dr. Billy Taylor, who wrote "I Wish I Knew How It Would Feel to Be Free." This program was for inner-city kids, and it was free, so we came from all the New York City boroughs for classes. The piano players would be in a class, the woodwind players in a class, and the brass players in a class. At the end, we would come together in the big band setting and play stock arrangements of Dizzy Gillespie, Count Basie, Duke Ellington, and Oliver Nelson. Paul was my teacher, and I remember how he made me feel special, like, "You can do this. Don't worry about a mistake. Turn it into something. Keep going. Don't give up." He really planted that in my head. "It's already in you. You just have to believe. Don't be afraid." That was Paul.

MICHAEL GREIF ON JOE PAPP

I had the unbelievable privilege of knowing Joseph Papp (founder of Shakespeare in the Park and the Public Theater) for a short time at the end of his life. I worked closely with him, and I saw the kind of theater he was making. I saw the incredible way in which he believed theater makes community, and helps us understand each other better. He was probably the biggest professional mentor in my life.

KRIS DIAZ ON MICHAEL DINWIDDIE

My mentor is Michael Dinwiddie, who was my teacher at NYU and is now my colleague there. He came to NYU when I was a junior, and he had the career that I wanted to have. He had done theater, he'd gone out to L.A. to work in TV a little bit, and he came back to teach. He was still doing all of that when I met him, so I saw that drive. Michael was also one of those people who, if you came in and said, "I would like to do this thing," he'd say, "Let's do it." And then he would walk me down the hall to somebody else's office to make the next step happen. There's a lot of Michael Dinwiddie in everything I do, and there's definitely a lot of him in the show.

MALEAH JOI MOON ON TIMOTHY WALTON

Timothy Walton was my high school theatrical director and vocal coach. The high school productions in our township were like our Broadway. Tim put his heart and his soul into each one, and it was always so inspiring, because it's obviously not Broadway, it's not even regional theater, but he cared so much about the students going through his academic training. He really funneled his creativity and artistic integrity into us. I remember him telling me, "Be a sponge, and don't be afraid to ask questions. Don't be afraid to sit in and watch, and don't be afraid to raise your hand when times call for raising your hand."

In high school, I did every show I could possibly do under Tim's tutelage. We did *RENT*, and I played Joanne. We did *West Side Story*, I was Maria. We were going to do *Dreamgirls* before the pandemic came, and I was going to play Deena. Two years after I graduated, the *Hell's Kitchen* audition came along. I was struggling to learn the material. All we had was sheet music; there were no plunk tracks, and I don't play piano. I called Tim and said, "Can I come to your house?" He said, "Of course, come at three o'clock." I went over, and I'm sitting there on the couch holding his baby on my lap while he's at his piano, and we're just going over "Kaleidoscope" and just plinking out the melodies.

He's a big pillar of the way that I look at my art as a 22-year-old on Broadway.

REDISCOVERING A SONGBOOK

3

This page: Alicia at a reading in 2019
Previous page: Tom Kitt and Adam Blackstone during rehearsal

WELCOME TO ALICIA LAND

By 2017, Alicia, Kris, and Michael had spent two years refining the story's characters, focus, and key emotional beats. Now it was time to lock in the next layer of storytelling: the music.

But which songs? Alicia was already working on her seventh studio album at this point; the first six contained more than one hundred tracks, many of them chart-toppers in both the U.S. and internationally. Alicia called for backup: musician and producer Adam Blackstone, her musical director for more than a decade.

Alicia Keys
Adam's a powerful musician and artist. We've done a billion different arrangements of songs and created special moments together. I knew it would be exciting to bring him into this project, because of his intimate knowledge of music overall, and then definitely his knowledge of my music. He really gets it.

Adam's schedule is always full. He's been music director for acts such as Nicki Minaj, Justin Timberlake, Maroon 5, and Rihanna, and he's done everything from Super Bowl halftime shows to Grammy and Oscar awards segments. In spite of his limited time, exploring a new medium appealed to him, and, as he says, "Alicia Keys doesn't take no for an answer."

Adam Blackstone, music supervisor and co-orchestrator
It's hard to say no to her, because her genius is so impactful. I also said yes because of what her music has meant to me, and I wanted it to mean something to somebody else in the same way.

Now, I gotta be honest, at first there was a little bit of musical-theater prejudice. You have these two strong, I gotta say it, musical geniuses, and we are very confident in what we do. So when we were told, "Oh, my God, you can't do that," or "This is how we did it for this show or that show," I said, "Yo, but that's not what my boss wants. That's not what I want. And I promise you, we are transcending Broadway. You gotta trust me." I said that for about three years.

Along with Michael and Kris, the pair met repeatedly at Alicia's Jungle City Studios office to determine which songs could advance and expand the storytelling. They ended up with twenty-two musical numbers: There were songs everyone knew had to

Adam Blackstone at a reading in 2019

be included, many reconfigured in unexpected ways; songs that couldn't quite fit (no matter how hard they tried); and then, where Alicia's vast songbook somehow fell short of dramaturgical needs, four new songs.

As the Public Theater's Oskar Eustis notes, the best-known songs bring an additional layer of audience experience to the show: Theatergoers are feeling the music as an organic part of the storyline, but they're also aware that it is the very caliber of music that Ali's character will go on to create.

Oskar Eustis, artistic director, Public Theater
Not only does the audience know what's going to happen to Ali, but they are reminded constantly by the songs. The music is actually the embodiment of her inner voice that she has not yet figured out how to make real in the world. What a great role for music to play.

THE MUST-HAVES AND THE WISH-WE-COULDAS

Kris Diaz, book writer
I had never written a musical but I'm a musical theater guy, and songs have to fit with the emotional beats of the story. We've got five or six of the greatest pop R&B songs ever written, in addition to a bunch of other fantastic songs. But "Fallin,'" "No One," "Girl on Fire," "If I Ain't Got You"—you've got to do all that. So we talked a lot about where those were going to live. Are we starting with "Empire State of Mind" or are we ending with "Empire"?

Alicia Keys
There was no way in the world we were gonna do this show without "Empire." It's the song people are waiting for, and especially once the show moved to Broadway, to be at the Shubert in that city on that street and in that neighborhood—literally in the Hell's Kitchen neighborhood—watching *Hell's Kitchen* and hearing "Empire," there's just nothing like it. So that was a no-brainer.

Mandy Hackett, co-producer
The first time I heard "No One" in context of the show, I cried. The tears were streaming down my face, and I remember thinking, *Oh my God, we're sitting on the biggest surprise when people start to hear these songs in this context, how elastic Alicia's music can be to fit different storylines*.

Alicia Keys
We knew "No One" was going to hold a place it never held before. You've always thought of it as lover to lover. You, for sure, have never thought of it as a

Adam Blackstone and Alicia working on the music

Alicia at a 2018 reading

Shoshana Bean (Jersey) and Brandon Victor Dixon (Davis) rehearsing "Not Even the King/Teenage Love Affair"

mother singing to a child, a child singing to a mother. Considering there's no bond deeper than parent and child, it's so beautiful when you hear those words, "You and me together through the days and nights. I don't worry, because everything's going to be alright."

"You Don't Know My Name" became a way to poke fun at Ali. Her homegirls are making fun of her for never having talked to this guy but having all these fantasies about him. It was so comical. It makes me laugh every time I see the show.

Possibly the most challenging song to distinguish from its original incarnation was "Fallin,'" Alicia's first hit single, from 2001. "Fallin'" earned her three Grammy Awards (Song of the Year, Best R&B Song, Best Female R&B Vocal Performance), and it is still, after all these years, generally considered one of her top three songs.

Michael Greif, director

We had an earlier version where Jersey was singing "Fallin'" and it felt wrong. We didn't want her to re-fall in love with Davis; that seemed like a terrible detour. Kris is the one who said, "Let's give it to Davis."

Kris Diaz

The script has a secondary love story of the mom and dad, but it was a complicated one. We figured out relatively early that "Fallin'" could live in that story. Once Brandon took it on, the beginning of the song turned into this extravaganza. I've seen him hold that opening line for forty-five seconds. By the end, every single person in the audience is feeling like, *I might be pregnant, I don't know, but I'm in love with him.*

That song also gave us permission to do a crazy thing structurally, which was put him in the show for two and a half minutes in the first act, and then have him show up for twenty minutes in the second act, take over, and then leave again. We wondered, *Can we do that?* And then we realized, that's the Davis experience. He drops in. He's everything. And then when you fall in love with him, he's gone.

Adam Blackstone

Alicia sat me down and said, "How would Sammy Davis Jr. sing 'Fallin'?" I said, "Well, let me get off the piano. Sammy would do it like this." And I got on the upright bass and started doing a little bit of swing. She said, "Oh my God, that's it."

Alicia Keys
"Fallin'" is not usually heard with a male voice. Also, we gave it this very jazzy feel. The chorus becomes double time, and everything about the verses has Davis prowling around Jersey. He knows that she really is attracted to him but doesn't want to be. So he delivers this sensuality and this playfulness, and it's almost too far, but then it's not. It's funny, it's serious, it's dramatic, it's sensual, it's all of it.

When you have songs that are so well known, people want to hear things the way they know them. That makes it difficult, the push and pull between what people want and you bringing them to a new place. It was so exciting to reconstruct these songs with Adam. I think you can only do that with somebody who is intimately familiar with the material. One of the things we both love is when people say, "I've never thought of the music in this way before."

In the song-spotting process, creative teams consider dramatic needs but also pacing and audience experience. It's a complex matrix, and even some beloved songs didn't make the cut. An original song Alicia wrote for Jersey didn't make it. Chris Lee wished that Knuck and his fellas could have had a bonding moment with "Underdog"; Adam campaigned for "Diary," one of his personal favorites; and Michael suggested "When It's All Over," which was in the show for a time.

Alicia Keys
"When It's All Over" was amazing. We had it right after Ali has come to terms with Knuck leaving. It was really strong. Eventually, to cut time, we removed it. But, man, that was hard, and everybody missed it so much it ended up on the cast album.

Four new songs from Alicia, with Adam's arrangements, debuted in *Hell's Kitchen*. The spirited "Seventeen" replaced the earlier song Alicia had written for Jersey.

Alicia Keys
We needed a song for Jersey that expressed why she had to make sure Ali was good. It needed to be punchy and dramatic. It needed to be over-the-top. I literally dreamed "Seventeen," and wrote it at the very end, right when people were saying, "Uh, where's the song? We need the song." I love the rhythmic cadence of it. I love how big it is and how boisterous Jersey gets to be.

Adam Blackstone with Aaron Romero on bass during rehearsal

The other three original songs in the show are "River," "Hallelujah/Like Water," and "Kaleidoscope."

Alicia Keys
"Kaleidoscope" was for sure written and born for this moment. It's about when your whole world turns upside down and you are swept up in the kaleidoscope. It has distinctive opening measures that are super simple, but you immediately feel good. It has these big vocals in it, big voices, big harmonies, it goes almost gospel soul, but it starts off like a perfect pop song. It speaks to what Ali is feeling in the moment she meets Miss Liza Jane, so we needed something that was going to completely stand out, where everything became this gorgeous color to express her awakening.

EVERYBODY PITCHES IN

Mandy Hackett
One day I walked into the rehearsal room and Alicia was teaching the music to the cast herself, note by note. She continued to do this through all our developments at the Public, all through rehearsal, all through to Broadway.

Monet, associate director
Alicia would come in and teach the vocal parts church-style. She'd sing a line and then have the person sing it back to her. It is that level of care, involvement, and collaboration that made those songs the way that they are.

More pieces fell into place when Adam called in pianist Erskine Hawkins to help lead vocal rehearsals, and Alicia recruited Vanessa Ferguson (Tiny), who knew a bit about Alicia's process from her experience on *The Voice*. Vanessa, along with Chris Lee, naturally fell into a leadership groove.

Kris Diaz
Vanessa and Chris both played such a big part in helping everybody understand all the music. They always knew everybody's vocal lines.

Chris Lee, actor (Knuck)
I'm a musician, so I always remembered the music. Kind of out of nowhere, Alicia started calling Vanessa and me section leaders. Each reading we remembered everything, and so then we would end up teaching. Eventually we were hired as voice captains.

Alicia Keys
Those two are my babes. She was an alto, and he was a tenor, but they understood all the parts, which was needed, because you're teaching it over and over again to different people and in different capacities. I could go away for two weeks, come back, and it didn't

Maleah Joi Moon (Ali) and ensemble members at rehearsal

Vanessa Ferguson (Tiny) and Chris Lee (Knuck) during a 2019 reading

fall apart because Chris and Vanessa understood how it's supposed to feel and sound. They both come from worlds of multiplicity: R&B, soul, hip-hop, jazz. They're able to flow through all of it. A lot of people can do only one thing.

To complete the show's music, still more special forces were needed, including an orchestrator, a music director, and a sound designer.

Mandy Hackett
Normally, on a musical, there's a composer, and the composer writes everything down. There's sheet music. There's a book. But Alicia was teaching the music. Whenever she was not there in person, Adam would be there. Erskine was always there. Nothing was written down, but now we were starting to build the bigger ensemble numbers. We were going into rehearsal, and we really needed to build out the music team, which meant bringing on orchestrators and copyists.

Monet
I did a little translating sometimes between the Public and Alicia and Adam, including after the Public told them they needed to bring in an orchestrator. I happened to be grabbing something from the room they were in, and they asked, "Monet, what is this? Why do we need an orchestrator?" They didn't like it because in their space, they are the orchestrators. They were like, "Well, we're gonna do it." I said, "Yeah, you're gonna do it, but do you want to also write the entire guitar book?" They said, "No," so I was like, "We need somebody to do that."

Mandy Hackett
The summer before we went into rehearsal, I literally woke up in the middle of the night and said, "Oh my God, it's Tom Kitt." I remember thinking, *Can I text Tom now?* It was three or four in the morning. I texted him the next day, and I remember saying to him, "Nothing is written down. Literally nothing is written down."

Tom Kitt, music consultant
The summer of 2023, I went to a Public Theater Gala in Central Park. Maleah Joi Moon and Brandon Victor Dixon performed "If I Ain't Got You." I was in the audience, and it was so mesmerizing and beautiful. I remember being so enamored and excited and thinking, *How can I be a part of that?* Literally the next day, Mandy Hackett called me. She said, "Do you know we're developing *Hell's Kitchen*?" I said, "Of course, I saw the performance last night." She asked if I would be interested in potentially joining the music team. I said I would be thrilled.

WHAT ADAM HEARS

Alicia Keys's longtime collaborator and music director, Adam Blackstone, on what he hears in the voices of the original Broadway cast.

When Alicia and I heard **Maleah Joi Moon** for the first time, our mouths dropped to the ground. Michael was looking at us like, *I told you*. She sang "The River." I never worked with Whitney Houston. I never worked with Michael Jackson. But I would say I've worked with everybody since then, and I've never heard anybody be able to have as much voice control while she's doing other things, climbing a scaffold, dancing, getting undressed, getting dressed, eating. I've never heard her hit a wrong note. She is a bona fide star. It's not a fluke. She captivates you from the first minute.

"I'VE NEVER HEARD HER HIT A WRONG NOTE."

Shoshana Bean came in with that soul, that grit, the expertise of knowing voice-to-chest-to-head voice, and then being able to mesh the pop world with the Broadway world. What I've learned in these last couple years is that not a lot of people are able to do that crossover well. Shoshana brought that from minute one.

I first saw **Brandon Victor Dixon** in *Jesus Christ Superstar* with John Legend. They're both quiet assassins and just so professional. It seems to me that Brandon sings better and better every day. He's able to do amazing things with his voice. A lot of artists don't have that connection from brain to throat to tell it what to do. He can literally tell his voice what to do.

When **Kecia Lewis** got on stage for our first day, I was like, *Whoa*. She's one of the people in this realm who's taught me how much dialogue and song can drive a story. As a pop guy, I have been trying to recreate theater on the pop concert stage for a while, from Kanye West to Alicia to Justin Timberlake, but there's no dialogue. When you get the dialogue happening with a song lyric, there's nothing like it, and Kecia brings that home every time.

Chris Lee brings '90s Jodeci meets Boyz II Men, but he also has this incredible teddy bear sensibility. I loved his work ethic. I love the fact that he was also willing to push the boundaries for the character.

Tom Kitt and Alicia Keys during rehearsal

Brandon Victor Dixon singing at a rehearsal in 2023

Mandy Hackett
Tom Kitt met with Adam and Alicia and then came on as the music consultant and co-orchestrator. Tom built some of his career working with Green Day on *American Idiot* and with Alanis Morissette's songs in *Jagged Little Pill*, so he had worked with singer-songwriter legends. He plugged right into the music team and was able to help Adam and Alicia think about not just the songs, but also music for when scenery is changing and how to orchestrate the music once the show went to Broadway.

Since no sheet music existed, Tom immediately got to work on creating the piano vocal book, which serves as a core reference for the entire team. He collaborated with Adam on expanding the orchestration.

Tom Kitt
My job is helping a score like this find its way as a musical, making sure everything feels authentic and in the world of the show. And I think everyone was nervous about what enhancing the orchestration—adding strings and horns to songs that never had them—would feel like, and whether that would in any way compromise the authenticity of the music.

Adam Blackstone
The genius of Tom was that he didn't try to change the orchestration Alicia and I had come up with. He just wanted to enhance it, and that's why we fell in love with him. That's my brother forever now.

Alicia Keys
Tom's orchestrations are so beautiful. I love how he took the time to think about, *How is this supposed to feel?* It was important that we kept the rawness and the New York energy. Adam and I were clear about how we wanted it to sound, and Tom adopted that vision and brought it to life.

Tom Kitt
Many of the arrangements were already in motion by the time I came on board that summer. I was so blown away by how it was fully a musical, because I've been on shows where it's a challenge to use songs that have been written in a different context. When I got there, I got to ask questions and come in with some new ideas. But I also knew I was going to learn so much from Alicia and Adam's artistry. It's been a wonderful learning process because we all hear different things. Seeing what they pinpoint to work on has definitely shaped the way I now hear music.

BRINGING THE MUSICAL TO LIFE: SOUND DECISIONS

Brandon Victor Dixon, actor (Davis)
This is Alicia's vision and it's Alicia's music, but she was really aware that a musical requires a community to bring it to life. She was very engaged in figuring out how her music existed on our voices and on our bodies. For us as artists, it was easy to sing this music, because great music receives other voices with tremendous ease.

Kris Diaz
My favorite thing during rehearsals was watching people watch Brandon. There is something magical

Kecia Lewis singing during a 2023 rehearsal

Aziza Miller on the keys

when he starts playing with songs. Throughout all the workshops, everybody felt that freeness, whether it was Kecia or Chris or Maleah. You would watch the other singers and dancers flip out every time somebody did a new run or riff. There were jokes about taking off shoes and throwing them at people. I would get up and throw my hands up and walk out of the room because somebody just did a crazy riff. We created a space, and it started with Alicia, where people could jump in and experiment and everybody was supportive of it.

Chris Lee

When Maleah and I sing together, it's peanut butter and jelly, and that's about more than vocal talent. Maleah is a phenomenal singer, but she's also got a crazy musical ear. She is willing to listen and sing at the same time. I'm very much like that as well, so most of the time, we're looking to serve each other rather than take our moment to show off. We're playing ping-pong. We're not playing keep-away, and we're not playing tag.

Kris Diaz

We were all sitting in the room when Kecia dropped down in "Authors of Forever" for the first time. She sings the line "made to survive," and "survive" goes, like, through the basement. People were staggered by it. It was like watching Michael Jordan play basketball.

For Alicia, Broadway's music scene was more regimented than she was used to, filled with rehearsal time limits and entrenched job descriptions. Some of these conventions were designed to offer worker protections, but their flip side was to limit creative possibilities.

Alicia Keys

In music, everyone belongs everywhere. But in theater, it's very clear: If you're the stage manager, you're the stage manager. If you're the actor, you're the actor. Everyone does their job, and it fits into the bigger whole. But that makes it difficult for new energy to be welcomed into the space. Adam and I were asking, "Where are the musicians? Where is the diversity, where's the vibe, where's the energy?"

One person we were looking for was a pianist who could support the Miss Liza Jane character musically. It had to be a person who could play the blues, classical, stride piano, jazz, and soul, and we wanted that person to be visible from the stage. When I tell you this pot was already small, it got smaller than it's ever been. I was like, "Should we not have the person onstage playing? No, we have to see a Black woman playing piano. We have to." One day an idea dawned on me, and I was like, "Well, could this work?"

Aziza Miller, Alicia's high school music teacher
I received a video chat from Alicia, and she described this project she'd been working on for thirteen years, and then she asked me, would I be a part of it? Her vision was for me to be seen and to actually play the featured numbers for the Liza Jane character that's loosely based on our mentor-student relationship.

I called her back and said, "Well, Alicia, I would love to do this, but I'm retired, and I don't know if I can keep up with that Broadway pace." And Alicia said, "You need to come out of retirement. You can do this."

If I'm passionate about something, I'm unstoppable. Aches and pains? What aches and pains? I'm happiest when I'm fulfilling my purpose. And when a person knows where their purpose is, man, it's not work. It's your calling, So my own words came back to me: "Don't let your fear of failure prevent you from trying." That's been my life. I said, "Well, if I tell my students that, I gotta follow my own advice."

Alicia Keys
I knew that for the story itself, if this could happen, energetically, karmically, it was the right thing. Miss Aziza had given me so much, and could I, in turn, give her a piece of what she had given me?

Aziza Miller
This is what we call a full-circle moment. It's special to be remembered. She never forgot me for my influence, and I never forgot her, either. She's my daughter in music. I love how she's blossomed. She's a mature, beautiful young woman, a wife, a mother, and she remembered her mother of music right here. And I'm so grateful, because the truth is, I wasn't ready to retire.

Two key spots on the music team were music director and sound design. For music director, Tom suggested Lily Ling.

Lily Ling, music director
I'm a Chinese-Canadian immigrant and a classically trained pianist, but I grew up listening to Alicia's music, so I was glad to meet with her and Adam. Alicia asked me a question that I have never been asked: "What would it mean to you to do the show?" I said, "I have never executed, as a music director, a big Broadway show by a female composer. To be able to execute music written by someone I've admired would be really amazing." On Broadway currently, I'm still the only music director who hits the intersection of both female and non-white.

Alicia Keys
I was so excited to meet Lily, a woman of color who is so dynamic and able to lead in a beautiful way. As the

The sound booth at the Shubert

Lily Ling conducting singers for the Original Broadway Cast Recording

musical director and the conductor, you have to lead not only the ensemble, but the entire cast. There's a confidence that has to be there. There's a rhythm, a stability, and a power to command attention that has to be there. And at the same time, Lily's playing so many of the piano parts. It felt right, and it felt like the representation that I've been dreaming of for this project. It's her job to keep the show together musically. And she really does that.

One of Lily's great pleasures is playing piano with the band, which is spread out across five locations, four of them visible onstage.

For such a complex production to work, extraordinary technology is required. A camera is trained on Lily as she conducts and plays, and the video feed goes out to every musician. From the stage, the cast can see two "conductor-cam" screens hanging from the balcony, and the sound board and stage manager have the same feed offstage. Lily also has foot-pedal-operated talkback mics for when she wants to speak to the band or the stage manager. Even more extraordinary, Lily says, is how fully her band is in sync.

Lily Ling

Most shows have had the edges shaved off the original music, and it's been musical-theaterized. In *Hell's Kitchen*, when we really are making music, we have to listen to each other, as opposed to playing to the click of a metronome. "Unthinkable" is one of those songs that is the opposite of having a metronome going. There's this moment in the middle of the song where suddenly the bass comes in. There's a boom, and you feel the entire building reverberate with this big bass drum that's played by our percussionist, Víctor Pablo. When we play that together, he and I are the only two people in the building who play that *boom, two, three, doom, doom*. It's not metronomic. We're a floor apart, but we feel it, and we feel it and breathe it with the actors as well.

Another dimension of the show's sonic experience comes from British sound designer Gareth Owen, one of the few non–New Yorkers on the creative team.

Gareth Owen, sound designer

I'm responsible for the communication systems that allow everyone to talk to each other. Then there is making the band sound good, making the vocal sound good. There's also all the sound effects. There's the surround sound. There's the vocal processing to make a tired singer still sound like a million bucks. So much of it is making sure other people can do their jobs properly.

BUCKET DRUMMING

In the show's opening number, "The Gospel," actors and dancers fill the stage with the street energy that's so enticing to seventeen-year-old Ali. What catches her attention most, though, is the three young men who set up their five-gallon buckets on a front corner of the stage. Ali's mom—and much of the rest of society—may see the trio through a lens of "drugs, guns, thugs," but their intention is purely self-expression, joy, and camaraderie. And the three drummers are following the long-standing tradition of making a way out of no way.

"Instruments manifest out of whatever you have at your disposal," says the show's percussionist, Víctor Pablo García-Gaetán, who played on Saltine tins when he was a child. "Bucket drumming is credited to a guy in New York named Larry Wright in the '70s and '80s. The sound at that time, what the buckets are emulating, is a lot of kick, a lot of snare. Having that tension and release, that's what all music is about."

Monet, associate director

We knew we needed to have bucket drumming with the characters Knuck, 'Riq, and Q. Before our first workshop, Adam asked if we could we bring somebody in, so the Public hired a bucket drumming specialist, Jared Crawford, and he came to vibe with the boys and figure out what was possible. We had to put together a presentation for the choreographer the next day, so I spent that night looking at videos online, and I put together a structure for the drumming. I was thinking, *This will do for now. Surely Adam at some point is gonna be like, "This is not what I want."* But that never happened. Chris Lee made what we sketched out look good, and it stayed forever.

Chris Lee, actor (Knuck)

This ended up being one of my favorite parts about the role. If you were tired that day, if you were hungry, if you were going through some heartache, whatever it was, once you started, *ka ka kak boom*, you were in it. You are completely thrown in from the second "Yeah Yeah Yeah."

Lily Ling, music director

Music is such a huge part of the lives of these young Black men, but what they're doing is not seen as high-class. If they showed up with a concert snare drum, it would be very different, but because it is a bucket drum, it is seen as disturbing the peace, which just shows society's prejudices about what music is and isn't. What is so beautiful in "Gospel" is that by featuring bucket drumming, we're sending the message that it is integral, that it has musical and artistic value.

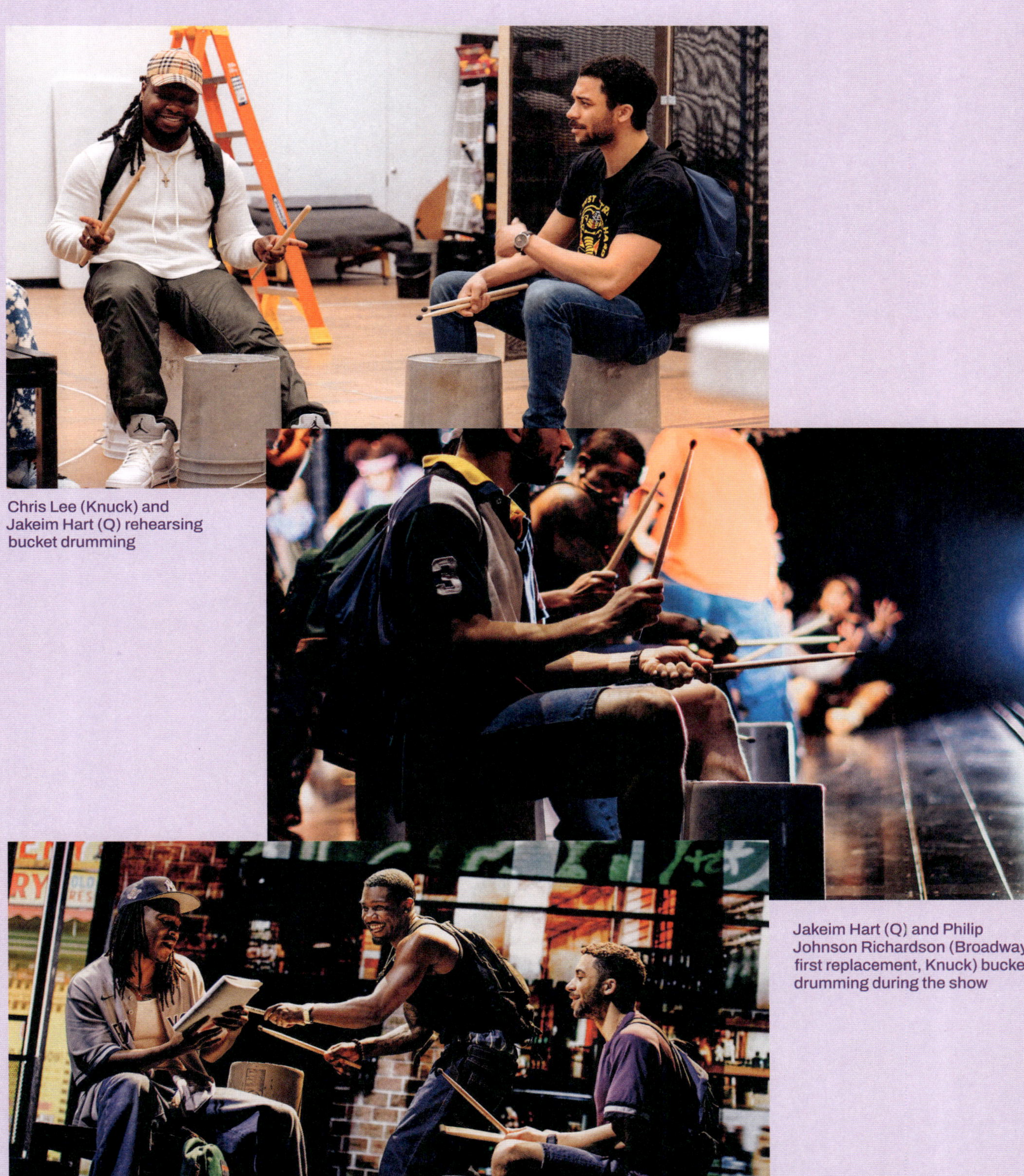

Chris Lee (Knuck) and Jakeim Hart (Q) rehearsing bucket drumming

Jakeim Hart (Q) and Philip Johnson Richardson (Broadway first replacement, Knuck) bucket drumming during the show

Lamont Walker ('Riq), Philip Johnson Richardson (Broadway first replacement, Knuck), and Jakeim Hart (Q) bucket drumming during the show

"The end of the dance break in 'Gospel' is the craziest sound moment I've ever heard in musical theater. They finish, and it just goes boom. It's like a nuclear bomb moves through the house."

Positioning musicians on the stage conveys the feeling of Manhattan Plaza as a hive of artists surrounding Ali, but that placement threatened to overwhelm the performers as well as the first few rows of the audience. The solution was to make most of the instruments electronic, so that they're actually silent onstage. The drum kit is electronic. The guitarists play into guitar cabinet simulators. Aziza Miller plays an electric keyboard built into the shell of a baby grand piano. The only instruments onstage that make noise are the drum set, the congas, and bongos.

Gareth Owen
One of my favorite sound effects is just before Kecia Lewis sings "Perfect Way to Die." The director said to me, "When the police arrest Knuck I want you to make something really aggressive, and you can do what you like." What I came up with is made of the screeching of metal and bending of sirens and this huge gran cassa bass drum that is mangled through distortion tools to make it really, really unpleasant. The whole thing hits you like an anvil in the chest. That is very much the intention. It's supposed to be jarring and offensive, almost, to the audience.

Alicia Keys
Gareth Owen was phenomenal. It's his mission to create a sonic experience that's going to feel full and powerful and big, and yet you still hear the nuances.

Gareth Owen
Alicia is a proper taskmaster. She's completely nocturnal, and she never stops. She never, ever stops. And so we'd get to the end of the day, eleven o'clock, and Alicia would be like, "Yeah, we're just going to stay behind and work on some sound and music stuff." And at two o'clock in the morning, we would still be sitting there. Like, does she ever stop? Does she ever run out of energy? But it was so rewarding. You know, it wasn't like she was keeping us there because she had nothing better to do. She was keeping us there because it was achieving great results.

Lily Ling
"Perfect Way to Die" is this ineffable moment that combines the character, the actor, the songwriting and orchestration, and the incredible brilliance of the sound design of Gareth Owen. What helps is the 808 bass that Víctor Pablo plays on the percussion pad. That's just *boom, boom* on every quarter note. That bass is the heartbeat of Miss Liza Jane and Ali coming together, their hearts uniting. With Kecia singing, all the elements come together—we hear the words, but we also feel the subwoofer speakers. This experience is what I would call one of the most perfect examples of theater magic.

Gareth Owen
We have two sets of subwoofers, one flown above the stage and one sitting along the front edge of the stage in what would normally be the orchestra pit. That was something we had to develop quite carefully in order to get what Alicia and Adam wanted. We're also using some quite cutting-edge technology that I was lucky enough to be involved in the development of: Each performer is wearing a tracker, and the tracker tells a computer system where they are onstage in three dimensions, and it assigns the sound to that spot.

Lily Ling directing musicians for the Original Broadway Cast Recording

Adam Blackstone
As the story developed, the music was also driving what was happening onstage, and then you couldn't deny the lyric. "Girl on Fire" was already one of your favorite songs ever, but now that we're putting it into the story context, it had to have Freddie Mercury drums. I said, it needs to go, *boom, ka-ke boom, boom*. I said, "Turn it up." I would yell in the theater, "Turn it up 8000 dB." They start laughing at me. But that's the feeling that we wanted to portray. Not that you're at a concert, because it's not that, but you want the same nostalgic feeling when you're watching it tell a different story.

Gareth's my guy. But from the start, I said, "Yo, number one, this has to sound and feel like New York. Number two, it needs to represent what Alicia Keys has sounded like for the last twenty-five years that has gotten her the acclaim she has gotten." Otherwise, we wouldn't be ourselves, we would be doing an adaptation, and that's not what this is. This is a direct representation, sonically, of where we wanted this to push the envelope, to be on Broadway, to open new doors for people like Maleah Joi Moon and Chris Lee and to bring in the Shoshanas that have been on Broadway but not been able to infuse themselves into the characters.

Kris Diaz
The end of the dance break in "Gospel" is the craziest sound moment I've ever heard in musical theater. They finish, and it just goes *boom*. It's like a nuclear bomb moves through the house. At the beginning of our Shubert run, that moment used to shake the building. There was leftover confetti around from a show that had been there years before and Gareth was shaking the building so much that during that number, all throughout rehearsal, we had confetti falling down.

Aaron Romero, Ben Weiss, and Marc Malsegna at the Original Broadway Cast Recording

Alicia Keys
It's a whole new universe where we are with sound. When we walk into that theater, it sounds so crystal and big and powerful and exciting and thrilling, and you're hearing from all different directions. Gareth understood how important it is for people to hear it and feel it. That's how they'll get connected to the story. Tom, Lily, and Gareth are three powerhouses, and I loved working with them.

THIS GIRL IS ON FIRE

"Girl on Fire" was the title track from Alicia's fifth album, released in 2012. When the song came out, it was praised for its anthemic quality, and it became known as a declaration of breaking through constraints and following one's passions. In *Hell's Kitchen*, the song gets a twist. Sung by one of Ali's homegirls, Jessica (Jackie Leon), the song feels more playful, more indulging of Ali's adolescent bravado. This was Jackie's one solo in the show, and it was a monumental experience for this Broadway first-timer.

Jackie Leon, actor (Jessica)
It was so nerve-wracking. The responsibility of this job is no joke. As an ensemble singer, we are singing the whole time backstage and onstage, but our mics aren't hot. There's a different weight when your mic is hot and the lights are on you. I remember Alicia said to me, "The energy you bring is fire."

Still, when we were at the Public, I'd get so anxious that I couldn't hold the final note all the way through. I kept running out of air. And two great actresses, Crystal Monee Hall and Mariand Torres, asked me, "Are you breathing?" I said, "Yes." And they were like, "Then it's in your head." I said, "No, no. I'm singing with my body, and I feel it." They're like, "Your mind leads everything. When you think, you won't make it, you will run out of air."

I remember that lesson. And I overcame it, and I started singing it long. And then the holiday season came, and suddenly my voice was wrecked. I was so hoarse. Everything was dry. I started going to vocal lessons and to ENTs to figure out, why am I not able to sing? My voice teacher asked me, "Are you drinking?" I was like, "Uh," and he was like, "Well, stop that." He said, "Are you doing anything else?" I was like, "No comment for legal reasons." And he was like, "Well, stop it." I was like, "Then what about my joy?" He's like, "Find other things to bring you joy." And I was like, "But what about the stress of life?" And he's like, "Get a stress ball." And so I stopped drinking, I changed my diet, I got a humidifier, and I drank water. All of this discipline that I wasn't doing before. It's been these little steps of overcoming. I overcame the mental hurdle, and then I overcame the physical hurdle.

If you want to consistently sing this song and be in the show and do the best of your ability, you have to be disciplined. And I make sure to remember how fun that song is and how joyous it is. When I put all this expectation on it, it robs me of that joy, which then is the antithesis of what I'm supposed to be bringing to the piece. Every few months I have to shed my old skin and find a new version of myself that sings that song.

Jackie Leon performing "Girl on Fire"

Team huddle during a 2024 rehearsal

WHO WAS YOUR MENTOR?

COLE COOK ON ALICIA KEYS

My biggest mentor has been my sister, Alicia. She's always pushed me to chase my dreams, which is something you see her do in everything she does. I've changed from thinking I wanted to be in gaming simulation and programming, and going off to college for it; to coming out of that and not knowing what to do; to being a model for a while. Then I thought I wanted to be in the studio, and she was able to open those doors for me. I realized that I love music, but it's not my lane. It's her lane, and I want my own. That sent me back to school. She sent me to school for filming, and then I was able to start my business, which I've been running ever since. She's always just been in the corner of, "How can I help?" And it's not in any other way besides just wanting to see me succeed. She's my mentor and my sister, but also my best friend.

When I was born, my father—our father—and Alicia weren't talking. They weren't on the best of terms. She was ten or eleven at the time and she made the decision, "I want my brother in my life," and she wrote a letter to our dad saying that. For her to make a decision like that at such a young age is just like, who does that? Who thinks about that? I picture myself in her shoes, and I could have been very bitter and just like, *I don't want anything to do with this person*. But she made it a point to connect, and every time I was in New York, our grandmother would make sure we'd find time to see her. Once I was old enough to travel with her, she took me on tour during my school breaks. We've always been attached. It all started with her.

MANDY HACKETT ON TONY KUSHNER

I knew playwright Tony Kushner's work: I had seen *Angels in America* when I was in college, and I was completely blown away, utterly blown away. Two years later, I was hired to be the dramaturg on his play *Slavs!* at New York Theatre Workshop, which was his first play in New York after *Angels*. I really got to know Tony then, and similar to Alicia, he had the drive for excellence, the immense intellect, and the work habits. There's a common theme in the artists I believe in the most: They have this enormous talent, but also the work ethic is just so there.

BRANDON VICTOR DIXON ON JACK WADDELL

I started studying with my voice teacher, Jack Waddell, when I moved to New York City for college. Jack taught me about perseverance and relentless positivity, which is a weird thing to say, because I'm the opposite of relentlessly positive. But Jack always kept a smile on his face, no matter what he was going through. Considering his path in the industry, he definitely faced many challenges, but Jack always had a real joy and appreciation for every opportunity he had. I think the lesson is, he reminds me to find joy and gratitude throughout the journey.

MONET ON PATRICIA CROTTY

In high school, I was a super nerd: AP Physics, AP Computer Science, studying for the LSAT. Then I did my first musical and decided, all of a sudden, that I was going to do theater. So I went to a very small school in Palatka, Florida, called Florida School of the Arts, where I met Patricia Crotty. She was my first acting teacher. She opened the door wide for me to fall in love with the theater. And she gave me a foundation that I will forever be thankful for. As my life and career have grown over the past twenty years, she's always been there. She is also one who's been down, stay down. She's white, but I've never had to shy away from talking about race with her, or about my more challenging academic experiences and projects. She loves this art form so fully, and she creates a path for those who are willing to be a part of this beautiful, special thing that we do. She is like family now, and I'm very thankful for her.

CHRIS LEE ON WAYNE BRADY

I was doing *Hamilton* in Chicago, and when our Aaron Burr, Josh Henry, was leaving, we were told he was being replaced by Wayne Brady. We all laughed. *Yeah, right, Wayne Brady.* We figured there must be another guy named Wayne Brady, because it's not going to be like, *Let's Make a Deal* Wayne Brady or *Whose Line Is It Anyway?* Wayne Brady. But it was. It was that Wayne Brady.

When Wayne first saw the show, he came up to me after and said, "Kid, you're crazy talented." He's not shy about telling me how blessed I am to have my gifts, and how I should be using them properly. Having that encouragement coming from this guy, a Black man in the industry, is cool, because nobody in my family does what I do. He's kind of an angel. I did my first TV pilot with him, his daughter is the first artist I ever produced music for that wasn't a friend, and he connects me to people whenever he can. He encourages me and calls just to check in. Doesn't miss a holiday, does not miss a Christmas, Halloween, Valentine's Day, or MLK Day. He's my brother slash father slash mentor. I have three kids now, and so much of how I raise them I modeled after watching him raise his daughter. He's my heart. I love that guy.

LILY LING ON MARY-MITCHELL CAMPBELL

I've spent my entire career holding my gender on one shoulder and my race on the other. Failure is really not an option when you're the first, right? You're breaking all these barriers, so you just *do*.

I've been in New York for two and a half years, and throughout my time here, Mary-Mitchell Campbell [music supervisor and director] has helped me navigate the Broadway music industry, whether it's through interpersonal issues or learning about the systems and policies. She's also my sponsor for my work visa, but we really bonded over our love of education and mentorship and the idea of paving a way for people who look like us. Any time I'm stuck in a situation, I'll ask her for her advice. When Tom Kitt reached out to me about becoming music director for *Hell's Kitchen*, I asked Mary, "Is this a good idea?" She said, "Yeah, I told Tom to call you. Do it."

THE LIBRETTO

ACT ONE

THE GOSPEL
THE RIVER
SEVENTEEN
YOU DON'T KNOW MY NAME
KALEIDOSCOPE

ACT ONE

ACT ONE

GRAMERCY PARK
NOT EVEN THE KING
TEENAGE LOVE AFFAIR
UNTHINKABLE (I'M READY)
GIRL ON FIRE
PERFECT WAY TO DIE

THE GOSPEL

ALL OF NYC IS SINGING TO YOU

GARETH OWEN, SOUND DESIGNER

"I thought bucket drums were just something you hit and it made a noise, but the way they play them in 'The Gospel,' the way they play them with the combination of sticks, parts of their hands, the way they hit them on the side and different places on the drum to make a different sounds is absolutely fascinating. It's a real instrument."

SONG: THE GOSPEL

ALI (to audience)
It's like all of New York City is singing to you.

A GROUP OF NEW YORKERS SING.

ENSEMBLE
Yeah yeah yeah yeah
Yeah yeah yeah yeah
Yeah yeah yeah yeah
Yeah yeah yeah
I said we're all God's children
Products of the ghetto
Mama cooked the soup
Daddy did the yelling

RAY
Uncle was a drunk
Cousin was a felon
And when he got pinched
He told them he wasn't tellin

MILLIE
Auntie was a cook
Her husband was a crook
'Cause every job he had
They be paying him off the books

'RIQ AND Q
Ghetto university knowledge is all it took
In the tenement I was listenin' to the hook

KNUCK
Change gon' come
Spirit of Sam Cooke
And when the feds comin'
Everybody be shook

KECIA LEWIS, ACTOR (MISS LIZA JANE)

"The way the life of the community explodes and comes at you in 'The Gospel,' that's exactly what it felt like being a kid in that neighborhood at that time. The bucket drumming, the dancing in the courtyard, the people singing and screaming at the top of their lungs."

JESSICA AND TINY
Now we doing life
Like Eddie Murphy and Martin
On the chain gang
I was singing into the coffin

CRYSTAL AND TINY
Roaches and the rats
Heroin in the cracks
Couldn't blame me
I'm just giving the facts

ALI
I'm tryna hit the top
Cuz the bottom ain't where it's at

ENSEMBLE
Everybody got a past
But you can never go back

ENSEMBLE
Ohh ohh ohh ohh ohh ohh ohh ohh
Ohh ohh ohh ohh ohh ohh ohh ohh
Yeah yeah yeah yeah
Yeah yeah yeah yeah
Yeah yeah yeah yeah
Yeah yeah yeah yeah

DANCE BREAK.

KNUCK AND FRIENDS PLAY THE BUCKET DRUMS. ALI WATCHES HIM, HEARTS IN HER EYES.

ALI AND ENSEMBLE (Call and response)
Ohh ohh ohh ohh ohh ohh ohh ohh
Ohh ohh ohh ohh ohh ohh ohh ohh
Ohh ohh ohh ohh ohh ohh ohh ohh
I'll tell it like it is
How we ever gon' live?

CRYSTAL AND MILLIE
If we ain't gettin' money
How we feedin' the kids?

KNUCK, 'RIQ, Q, AND RAY
It's a revolving door
When brothers be doing bids
I know it sound wrong
But the dope'll be what it is

ALI, JESSICA, AND TINY
Survival of the fittest
This poor girl the illest
Broke mirrors and black cats
Give me heebiegeebies

RAY
Life seems hard
But nothing ever come easy
Whatever's in the dark
Will always become the light
If you ain't in the battle
How you gon' win the fight

KNUCK
Gotta speak the truth
When I'm up in the booth
The streets be flyin' birds
But they don't be on the roof

ENSEMBLE
Poverty is a pain
Like you pulling a tooth
Told the streets don't let me go
Like I'm bishop in juice

JERSEY
Roaches and the rats
Heroin in the cracks
Couldn't blame me,
I'm just giving the facts

ALI
Tryna hit the top,
The bottom ain't where it's at

ENSEMBLE
Everybody got a past
But you can never go back

ALI AND ENSEMBLE (Call and response)
Ohh ohh ohh ohh ohh ohh ohh ohh
Ohh ohh ohh ohh ohh ohh ohh ohh

ENSEMBLE
Yeah yeah yeah yeah
Yeah yeah yeah yeah
Yeah yeah yeah yeah
Yeah yeah yeah yeah
Yeah yeah yeah yeah
Yeah yeah yeah yeah
Yeah yeah yeah yeah

JERSEY HAS ENTERED.
SHE'S HEARD ENOUGH.

JERSEY Enough!

EVERYONE STOPS.

Get upstairs.

TRYNA HIT THE TOP, THE BOTTOM AIN'T WHERE IT'S AT

THE RIVER

SONG: THE RIVER

ALI
I'm alone in a corner
Of a one room apartment
Dirty windows let the light in
Through my fingers
& make patterns on the carpet

Heavy footsteps on the ceiling
And the sirens in the distance
Drown the sound of playing children
I am alone here in a crowd of 7 million

I know there's more to life than this
'Cause something's calling me

So I'll follow the river
So I'll follow the river

ALICIA KEYS

"We needed an 'I want' song that describes the big feelings Ali has of wanting to catch the wind and dying to begin. That ended up becoming 'The River,' which contains this idea of following your dreams and following the river, and it's gonna carry you where you need to go."

I'm gonna catch the wind, 'cause I'm dying
To begin
So I'll follow the river

ENSEMBLE
Follow the river
Follow the river

ALI
There's a heartbeat out on these streets
There's a bonfire that set a light inside
of me
There's no army that can stop me
Watch how strong I'm gonna be
When they said I couldn't be

ALI, CRYSTAL, AND MILLIE
I know there's more to life than this
'Cause something's calling me

ALI	ENSEMBLE
So I'll follow the river	*Ahh*
So I'll follow the river	*Ahh*
I'm gonna catch the wind,	
'Cause I'm dying to begin	
So I'll follow the river	
	Follow the river
	Follow the river
	Yeah yeah yeah yeah
	Yeah yeah yeah yeah
	Yeah yeah yeah yeah
	Yeah yeah yeah
Follow the river	
	Follow the river
	Follow the river

ALI
I know there's more to life than this
'Cause something's calling me

She's Seventeen and Her Brain Just Don't Work

COLE COOK, ALICIA KEYS'S BROTHER

"'Seventeen.' I remember the first time I heard that song. Alicia played it for me during a flight. I went into the bathroom and listened to it, like, that was how I had to listen to the song. I think we've all been in that place of being seventeen, and now being slightly older, we understand what the mother is saying and understand that what she's talking about in it makes sense. I love that song. Love it."

JERSEY It's not cold. It's facts. And it's not only her. It's all of them.

SONG: SEVENTEEN

They're kids in grown up bodies. They're hormones in hoodies. But the rest of them are not my responsibility. She is.

JERSEY
She's seventeen
And her brain just don't work

RAY Come on now, Jerz—

JERSEY That's enough, Ray. Thank you.

Just seventeen
And she's a piece of work

MILLIE I know I did some dumb stuff when I was her age.

JERSEY
She's sassy, kinna nasty, gotta me feelin batty
Get my nerves a rackin,
Acting like you bad-n
Might need u a smack, don't make me send her packin'
No
She's just seventeen
And her brains just don't work

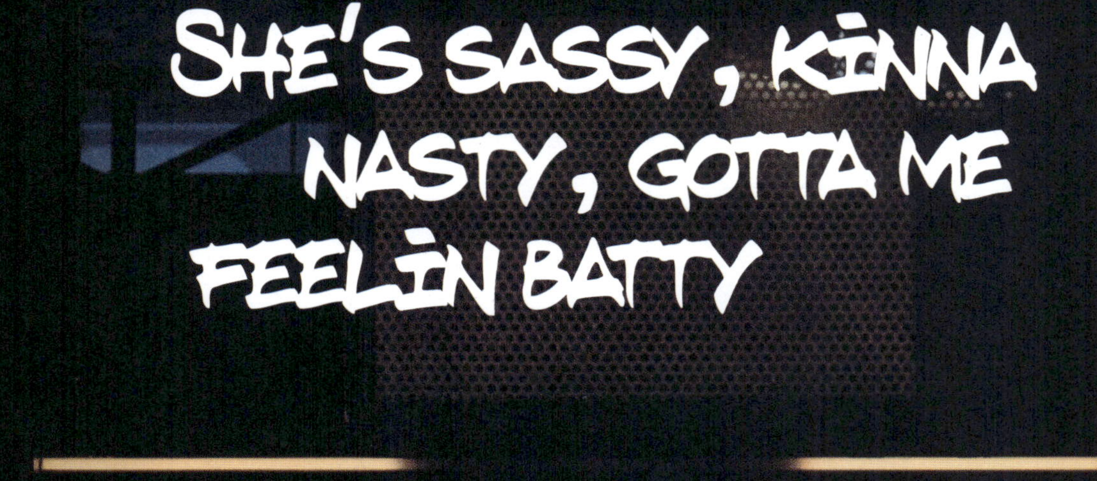
SHE'S SASSY, KINNA
NASTY, GOTTA ME
FEELIN BATTY

MILLIE With my kids? *Un chancletazo y se acabó.*

JERSEY
Think she knows it all

CRYSTAL
But she don't know nothing

MILLIE
All that's at stake she can risk

CRYSTAL
She can risk

JERSEY
I once was her
So I try to stop it
'Cause she 'bout to step in some shit

MILLIE
She'll feel the heat in the kitchen

CRYSTAL AND RAY
In the kitchen

CRYSTAL
Somebody is about to go missin

MILLIE AND RAY
Go missin

JERSEY
Testosterone and estrogen

CRYSTAL AND MILLIE
Estrogen

JERSEY
Bad combination

JERSEY, CRYSTAL, MILLIE, AND RAY
She don't never listen

JERSEY
She's sassy, kinna nasty, gotta me feelin batty
Get my nerves a rackin,
Acting like you bad-n
Might need u a smack,

JERSEY, CRYSTAL, MILLIE, AND RAY
Don't make me send her packin'
No oh no

JERSEY	**CRYSTAL, MILLIE, AND RAY**
She got me going loco,	
Never gonna fold so	*Ahh*
Put her in a choke hold	*Ahh*
That might stunt the mojo	
I'm a friend not foe	

JERSEY, CRYSTAL, MILLIE, AND RAY
Not gonna watch her blow
Oh, oh no

JERSEY	**CRYSTAL, MILLIE, AND RAY**
She pushes to the limit	
Might be at my limit	*Ahh*
She about to get it	
Hard place to sit in	*Ahh*
Imma have a fit	
Like she don't really know	*Ahh*
'Cause she's just seventeen	*Don't really know*
	Ha-ha, ha-ha, ha-ha
	Ha-ha, ha-ha, ha-ha
And her brain just don't work	*And her brain just don't work*

YOU DON'T KNOW MY NAME

ALICIA KEYS

"Tiny and Jessica and Ali together are En Vogue meets TLC. That's why, when you hear the way that they flip harmonies or they have that fun little diddy bop that they do, that's girl group energy."

JESSICA And you ain't about to step to him anyway. How long you been lookin in his direction?

TINY Forever.

JESSICA And you never introduced yourself yet.

TINY He don't even know you're alive.

ALI He will.

TINY Go ahead then!

JESSICA Make your move.

TINY Shoot your shot.

JESSICA You got so much game? Prove it. Walk on up to him and be like:

SONG: YOU DON'T KNOW MY NAME

JESSICA
Baby, baby, baby
From the day I saw you
Really, really wanted to catch your eye

TINY
Somethin' special 'bout you
I must really like you
'Cause not a lot of guys are worth my time

JESSICA
Oh baby, baby, baby
It's getting kind of crazy

TINY
'Cause you are taking over my mind

JESSICA
And it feels like

YOU'LL NEVER KNOW HOW GOOD IT FEELS TO HAVE ALL MY AFFECTION

JESSICA AND TINY
Ooh
He don't know your name

JESSICA
I swear

JESSICA AND TINY
She feels like ooh
He don't know your name

TINY
Round and round and round she go

JESSICA AND TINY
Will he ever know

ALI Oh, you think I won't?

JESSICA You won't.

ALI It's like you two don't know me at all.

ALI	JESSICA AND TINY
Oh, baby, baby, baby	
I see us on our first date	
Doing everything that makes me smile	
When we had our first kiss	*Ooh*
It happened on a Thursday	*Ooh*
Ooh it set my soul on fire	*Ooh*
Ooh baby, baby, baby	*Ooh*
I can't wait for the first	*Ooh*
time	*Ooh*
My imagination's running wild	*Ooh*
And it feels like	*Ooh*

ALI, JESSICA, AND TINY
Ooh
You don't know my name

TINY
Round and round and round we go

JESSICA AND TINY
Will you ever know

ALI Girl, I'm sayin': he don't even know what he's doin' to me. Got me feelin' all crazy inside. I'm feelin' like *oh*

AND YOU'LL NEVER
GET A CHANGE
TO EXPERIENCE
MY LOVIN'

...ARE YOU
TALKING TO
ME?

ALI	**JESSICA AND TINY**
Doing more than I've ever	*Ooh*
Done, for anyone's attention	*Ooh*
Take notice of what's in front of you	*Ooh*
'Cause did I mention (oh)	
You 'bout to miss a good thing	
And you'll never know	*Ooh*
how good it feels	*Ooh*
To have, all my affection	*Ooh*
And you'll never get a chance	*Ooh*
To experience, my lovin' (oh)	
'Cause my lovin' feels like	

ALI, JESSICA, AND TINY
Ooh
You don't know my name
And I swear on my mother and father it feels like

ALI	**JESSICA AND TINY**
Oh-oh-oh-oh-oh-oh-oh	*Ooooh*
Oh-oh-oh-oh-oh-oh-oh	*Ooooh*
Oh-oh-oh-oh-oh-oh-oh	*Round & round & round we go*

WHO ELSE WOULD I BE TALKING TO, SON?

KALEIDOSCOPE

Nights Like This They Belong in the Guinness

CHRIS LEE, ACTOR (KNUCK)

"I'll never forget the first time I heard 'Kaleidoscope,' just us singing it in rehearsal. There was no beat. It was just piano. And I was like, *This is the coolest song ever*. Alicia's so good, and she was right there, saying, 'It goes like this,' and then Adam Blackstone coming in and playing it on keys and adding stuff. I knew that was going to be everyone's favorite song."

ALI I walked in this room cold and wet and furious, but now? Nah, none of that matters. I knew something had been calling me. I think it might be her. I think it might be this.

SONG: KALEIDOSCOPE

ALI
Kaleidoscope
Tonight is shining bright you know
Oh yeah ohh no
So light it light it light it light it up
Put in the air and let it go
Oh yeah ohh no

Can you feel the love now
I'm feeling a buzz now
Never wanna come down
Piece it all together

Nights like this they belong in the Guinness
Nights like this never want them to finish
Don't wait for the end
Let's start a beginning
Better to be alive
Than just to be living

ALI
Nah nah nah nah nah
nah nah nah
Nah nah nah nah nah
nah nah nah

JESSICA, TINY, CRYSTAL, MILLIE
Hah hah hah hah hah
hah hah whoop
Hah hah hah hah hah
hah hah whoop

BRANDON VICTOR DIXON, ACTOR (DAVIS)

"'Kaleidoscope' is probably one of my favorite songs that Alicia's written, and it's one of the songs that really stands out in the show. I love the cultural influences you can hear in it."

ALI	**JESSICA, TINY, CRYSTAL, MILLIE**
Kaleidoscope	
Everyone looking high	*High*
and low	*and low*
Ohh yeah ohh no	
You're moving moving	
moving	
Way too slow	*Way too slow*
I think I got that antidote	*Antidote*
Oh yeah ohh no	
Can you feel the love now	*Love now*
I'm feeling a buzz now	*Buzz now*
Never gonna come down	*Come down*
Piece it all together	

ALI
Nights like this they belong in the Guinness
Nights like this never want them to finish
Don't wait for the end
Let's start a beginning
Better to be alive
Than just to be living

ALI	**JESSICA AND TINY**
Nah nah nah nah nah	*Ooooh*
nah nah nah	
Nah nah nah nah nah	
nah nah nah	*Ooooh*
Don't wait for the end	
Let's start a beginning	

DANCE BREAK.

ENSEMBLE
Ooooh
Ooooh
Ooooh
Ahhh

ALI	**ENSEMBLE**
Feels so good when it's	
all out	*All out*
Running through the	
dark til	
The sun's out	*Sun's out*
Maybe I am ready for	
the fallout	*Fallout*
I don't know what to say	

ALI	**ENSEMBLE**
(adlib riffing)	*It's a kaleidoscope*
	I see your colors baby
	Make a kaleidoscope
	With all your colors
	It's a kaleidoscope
	I see your colors baby
	Make a kaleidoscope
	With all your colors
	It's a kaleidoscope
	I see your colors baby
	Make a kaleidoscope
	With all your colors
	It's a kaleidoscope
	I see your colors baby
	Make a kaleidoscope
	With all your colors
	It's a kaleidoscope
	I see your colors baby
	Make a kaleidoscope
	With all your colors
	It's a kaleidoscope
	I see your colors baby
	Make a kaleidoscope
	With all your colors

11

GRAMERCY PARK

CHRIS LEE, ACTOR (KNUCK)

"Knuck gets one shot to matter in this show. And for me, that's 'Gramercy Park.' If you do not sell that moment, we do not care about the rest of the show. We do not care. I worked every night. I never phoned that in. I worked every night to be able to allow the audience to see the story of this guy who does not owe this girl an explanation but decides to give her one and kill two birds with one stone. One is, you've been bothering me, and I guess I'll let you know that. But also, it is nice to get this off my chest at the same time, right? He's like, *Yeah, what you think you see is not what it is.*"

SONG: GRAMERCY PARK

KNUCK
Are you gonna see me
When the light gets dark
The sun goes down over Gramercy Park
And it's become easy to hide pieces away
Making up someone in the hope that you'll stay
'Cause I been trying to be everything
I think they want me to be
I been doing all the things that
I think they wanna see
I been trying to fulfill them
With their every need
Now they're making me a person
That's not even me

KNUCK AND ENSEMBLE
Hmmm hmmm
Hmmm hmmm
Hmmm hmmm

KNUCK
Now they're making me a person that's not even me
Don't get me wrong
I wasn't out to deceive
I like the attention

Now they're making me a person that's not even me

With your eyes on me
The trouble with the truth is
It's so hard to believe
Now here I stand
With my heart on my sleeve
'Cause I been trying to be everything
I think they want me to be
I been doing all the things that
I think they wanna see
I been trying to fulfill them
With their every need
Now they're mak—

KNUCK BREAKS DOWN, THE EMOTION TOO MUCH TO BEAR. ALI CONSOLES HIM. HE LETS HER.

ENSEMBLE
Hmmm hmmm
Hmmm hmmm
Hmmm hmmm

KNUCK
Now they're making me a person that's not even me
Now you're falling for a person that's not even me
'Cause I forgot about the person
That I used to be

NOT EVEN THE KING

CHRIS LEE, ACTOR (KNUCK)

"The first time I heard Brandon sing the word 'money' in that line, 'Some people so poor, all that they've got is money,' I was like, Oh, my God. Come on. Let's just sit back. That moment is just hot buttery syrup on pancakes."

SONG: NOT EVEN THE KING

DAVIS ENTERS WITH AN UPRIGHT PIANO.

JERSEY Crystal and I had just finished doing I don't remember what show in I can't remember if it was Tompkins or—no, Seward Park, down on Essex Street—and this fool—your father—wheeled out this old upright piano and started to play.

JERSEY CAN'T TAKE HER EYES OFF HIM.

DAVIS
Money
Some people so poor
All that they got is money
Ohh and diamonds
Some people waste their life
Counting their thousands
I don't care what they're offering
How much gold they bring
They can't afford what we got
Not even the king
They can't afford what we got
Not even the king

Ohh castles
Some people so lonely
What good is a castle
Surrounded by people
But ain't got a friend
That's not on the payroll
Ohh and i don't care what they bring
They can have everything
They can't afford what we got
Not even the king
They can't afford what we got
Not even the king

JERSEY And all of a sudden, Davis and me were the only people in the world.

DAVIS
All the king's horses
And all the king's men
Came charging to get
What we got
They offered the crown
And they offered the throne
I already got all that I want
All the king's horses
And all the king's men
They came marching thru
They offered the world
Just to have what we got

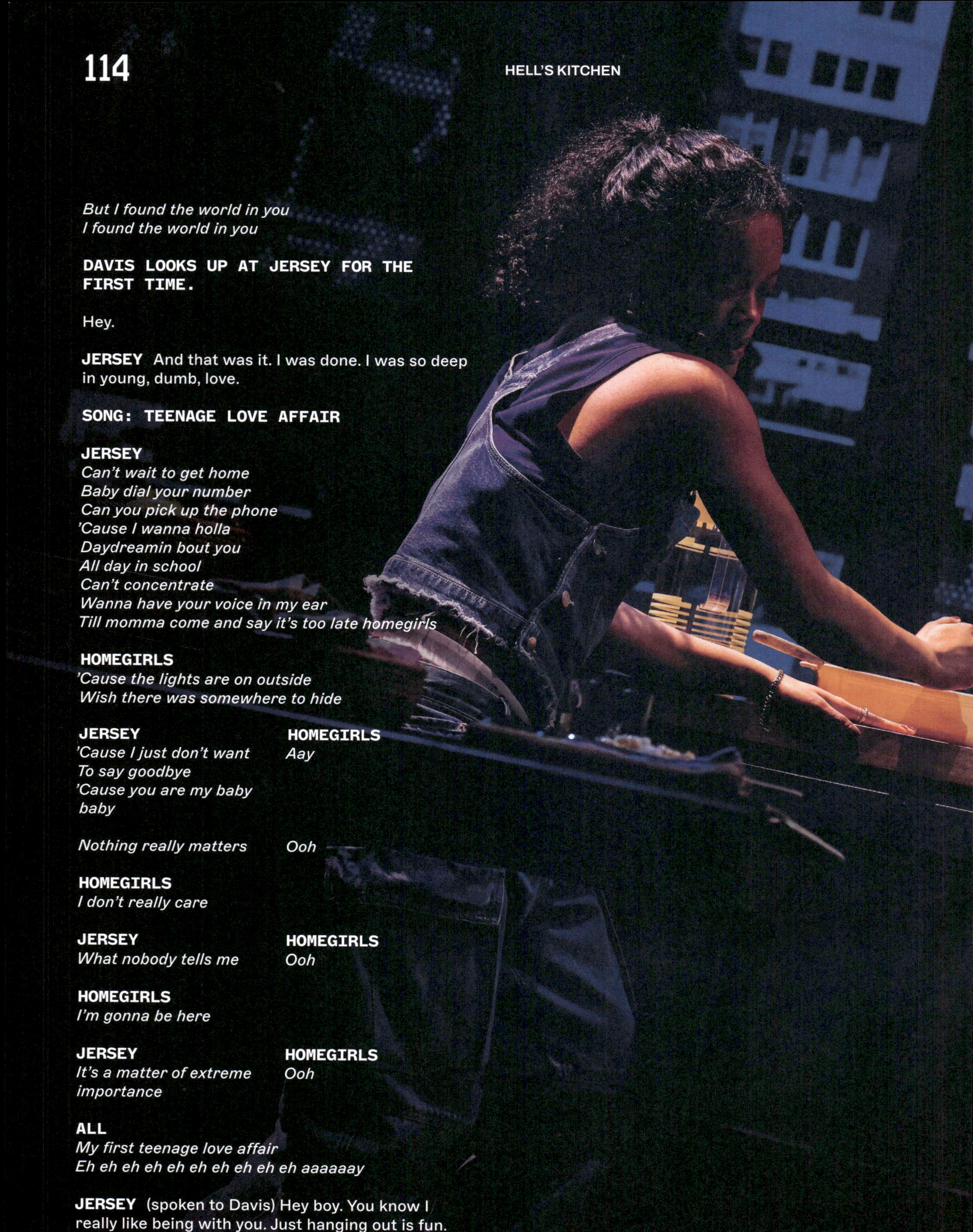

But I found the world in you
I found the world in you

DAVIS LOOKS UP AT JERSEY FOR THE FIRST TIME.

Hey.

JERSEY And that was it. I was done. I was so deep in young, dumb, love.

SONG: TEENAGE LOVE AFFAIR

JERSEY
Can't wait to get home
Baby dial your number
Can you pick up the phone
'Cause I wanna holla
Daydreamin bout you
All day in school
Can't concentrate
Wanna have your voice in my ear
Till momma come and say it's too late homegirls

HOMEGIRLS
'Cause the lights are on outside
Wish there was somewhere to hide

JERSEY	**HOMEGIRLS**
'Cause I just don't want *To say goodbye* *'Cause you are my baby* *baby*	*Aay*
Nothing really matters	*Ooh*

HOMEGIRLS
I don't really care

JERSEY	**HOMEGIRLS**
What nobody tells me	*Ooh*

HOMEGIRLS
I'm gonna be here

JERSEY	**HOMEGIRLS**
It's a matter of extreme *importance*	*Ooh*

ALL
My first teenage love affair
Eh eh eh eh eh eh eh eh eh aaaaaay

JERSEY (spoken to Davis) Hey boy. You know I really like being with you. Just hanging out is fun.

TEENAGE LOVE AFFAIR

SHOSHANA BEAN, ACTOR (JERSEY)

"This is my only moment, really, as Jersey, to be fun and playful."

JERSEY So maybe we can go to

HOMEGIRLS
First base

JERSEY
Because I feel you

HOMEGIRLS
Second base

JERSEY
Want you to feel me too boy

HOMEGIRLS
Third base

JERSEY
Better pump the brakes

We did not pump those brakes. And as a result, nine months later: we were parents. We were much too young to be parents, but we were parents. And for that moment at least, it was perfect.

SONG: NOT EVEN THE KING (REPRISE)

DAVIS
So darling listen
Your arms around me
Worth more than a kingdom
Yeah believe that
The trust that we feel
The kings never felt that

JERSEY AND DAVIS
Yeah this is the song we sing
We don't need anything
They can't afford this
This is priceless
They can't afford what we got
Not even the king
Can't afford what we got
Not even the king

I WAS WONDERING MAYBE
UNTHINKABLE
(I'M READY)

MONET, ASSOCIATE DIRECTOR

"No one was secretly doing all the lead producer work for Alicia. She was in the room all the time. When we got to 'Unthinkable,' we were trying to figure out staging for it, which was particularly tricky. Alicia was like, *Alright, let's try it this way. And what if we move this that way?"*

SONG: UNTHINKABLE (I'M READY)

ALI
Moment of honesty
Someone's gotta take the lead tonight
Who's it gonna be?
I'm gonna sit right here
And tell you all that comes to me
And if you have something to say
You should say it right now

KNUCK
You should say it right now

ALI AND KNUCK
You give me a feeling that I never felt before

ALI
And I deserve it, I think I deserve it

KNUCK
Let it go

ALI AND KNUCK
It's becoming something that's impossible to ignore

ALI
And I can't take it

ALI AND KNUCK
I was wondering maybe
Could I make you my baby
If we do the unthinkable
Would it make us look crazy
If you ask me I'm ready
If you ask me I'm ready
You give me a feeling that I never felt before

ALI
And I deserve it

KNUCK
I know I deserve it

ALI AND KNUCK
It's becoming something that's impossible to ignore
It is what we make it

ALI	**KNUCK**
I was wondering maybe	*Maybe*
Could I make you my	
baby	*Baby*
If we do the unthinkable	*Unthinkable*
Would it make us look	
crazy	*Crazy*
Or would it be so	
beautiful	*Beautiful*
Either way I'm saying	*I'm saying*

ALI AND KNUCK
If you ask me I'm ready
If you ask me I'm ready

KNUCK
Why give up before we try?
Feel the lows before the highs
Clip our wings before we fly away

ALI AND KNUCK
I can't say I came prepared
I'm suspended in the air
Won't you come be in the sky with me
I was wondering maybe
Could I make you my baby
If we do the unthinkable
Would it make us look crazy
Or would it be so beautiful
Either way I'm saying
If you ask me I'm ready
If you ask me I'm ready
If you ask me I'm ready
If you ask me I'm ready

THEY KISS. AND KISS.

NEW YORK
NYC

GIRL ON FIRE

SHE GOT BOTH FEET ON THE GROUND

JACKIE LEON, ACTOR (JESSICA)

"The funniest part of the show is Vanessa Ferguson walking onstage during 'Girl on Fire' and being like, 'Is this what we're doing, really?' And then her standing there going, 'I'm just saying,' and walking out of the building. Oh, it's so good. Or her rap, or when she does this, 'We're all gonna die.' I actually genuinely cackle at that part."

ALI She didn't say anything about Knuck. I think that means I got away with it! And I continue to get away it, for the next few weeks at least, and now? I got my mother under control, I got my love life on lock, kinda killing this piano thing already. Shoot. Now you can't tell me nothing.

KNUCK, PLAYING THE DRUMS, LEADS US INTO… SONG: GIRL ON FIRE

JESSICA
She's just a girl, and she's on fire

MILLIE
Hotter than a fantasy, lonely like a highway

JESSICA
She's living in a world,
And it's on fire

JESSICA AND MILLIE
Filled with catastrophe, but she knows she can fly away

ENSEMBLE
Oh, oh, oh, oh, oh

CRYSTAL
She got both feet on the ground
And she's burning it down

ENSEMBLE
Oh, oh, oh, oh, oh

KNUCK STARTS TO TEACH ALI TO PLAY THE BUCKETS.

'RIQ, Q, AND RAY
She got her head in the clouds
And she's not backing down

TINY Hold up. (Music stops.) The world is hers 'cause she got a man now? That's what we're doing?

JESSICA AND MILLIE...

TINY I'm just saying.

MUSIC RESTARTS.

ALI MOVES AWAY FROM KNUCK, INTERACTING WITH THE CITY ON HER WAY TO THE ELLINGTON ROOM. KNUCK, ON THE BUCKETS.

KNUCK
Looks like a girl, but she's a flame

KNUCK, 'RIQ, Q, AND RAY
So bright, she can burn your eyes
Better look the other way

ALI, ON THE BUCKETS.

KNUCK
You can try but you'll never forget her name

JESSICA, CRYSTAL, AND MILLIE
She's on top of the world

ALI STOPS DRUMMING, MOVES TO THE PIANO.

Hottest of the hottest girls say

ALI, ON PIANO. KNUCK, ON DRUMS.

ENSEMBLE
Oh, oh, oh, oh, oh

CRYSTAL AND MILLIE
She got both feet on the ground
And she's burning it down

KNUCK EXITS. ALI CONTINUES TO PLAY PIANO.

ENSEMBLE
Oh, oh, oh, oh, oh
She's got her head in the clouds
And she's not coming down

MISS LIZA JANE ENTERS AND TEACHES.

MISS LIZA JANE
Whole step. (Ali plays.)
Diminished. (Ali plays.)
Minor. (Ali plays.)
Alla breve!
Molto bene!

ALI PLAYS. MISS LIZA JANE APPROVES.

JESSICA
This girl is on fire
This girl is on fire

TINY "Alla breve?"

JESSICA	**ENSEMBLE**
She's walking on fire	*Fire Fire*
This girl is on fire	*Fire*

TINY Really?

ENSEMBLE
Oh, oh, oh, oh, oh
Oh, oh, oh, oh, oh
Oh, oh, oh, oh, oh

ALI AND JERSEY IN THE APARTMENT.

ALI She taught me classical. She taught me the blues. Tomorrow she's showing me Stevie!	**ENSEMBLE** *Ahh ahh*
JERSEY I love Stevie.	**ENSEMBLE** *Ahh*

ALI I know.

JERSEY You'll have to play for me sometime.

ALI I will! Have fun at work!	**ENSEMBLE** *Ahh*

JERSEY Thank you! See you for dinner.

JERSEY HEADS OUT.

ENSEMBLE
This girl is on fire
This girl is—

TINY Oh, hell no.

Yo Ali, you know I love you and I always keep it real
But you doing the most. You really need to chill.
So you feel like you're in love
And it's a really big deal
But are you thinking things through
It ain't about how you feel
And I don't mean to put your fire out
But when your mother finds out

TINY, 'RIQ, Q, AND RAY
She gone bring the whole empire out

TINY
I know you love the keys now like Stevie Wonder
But you was just in love with basketball last summer
And now you're saying that you so in love with this drummer
But what about your girls 'cause he's a newcomer
And you just gon break up the crew to leave us two
While you hanging out with him
What are we gonna do
You can't see clear 'cause you're falling in
This illusion of bliss
What y'all even got in common
Don't waste energy on this
Look
I love hanging out with you. We have a ball
But your mother...is gonna kill us...all...

Like we're all gonna die.

JESSICA Yeah, but—

JESSICA	**ENSEMBLE**
This girl is on fire	*Fire Fire*
She's walking on fire	*Fire*

ALI LEADS KNUCK INTO THE APARTMENT.

KNUCK I should not be here.

ALI She's at work. We got plenty of time.

KNUCK Yeah, but—

ALI Yeah.

ALI KISSES KNUCK. IT GETS MORE PASSIONATE. THEY UNDRESS.

JESSICA	**ENSEMBLE**
This girl is on fire	*Fire*

MICHAEL GREIF, DIRECTOR

"I remember sitting in 'Perfect Way to Die' rehearsals, feeling unbelievably privileged that I could be in the room with those feelings, that I was permitted entry into that story and that expression in that way between those two characters. At some point I said to Kecia, 'It's an honor for me to be allowed into this space.'"

MISS LIZA JANE Your rage is real. Your rage is earned. But I will not let you let it defeat you.

SONG: PERFECT WAY TO DIE

MISS LIZA JANE I will not allow you to let the pain win.

MISS LIZA JANE
Simple walk to the corner store
Mama never thought she would be
Getting a call from the coroner
Said her son's been gunned down
Been gunned down
Can you come now
Tears in her eyes
Can you calm down
Please ma'am can you calm down

It rained fire in the city that day
They say
A river of blood in the streets
No love in the streets
Then came silence in the city that day
They say
Just another one gone
And they tell her move on
And she's stuck there singing

Baby don't you close your eyes
'Cause this could be our final time
You know I'm horrible at saying goodbye
But I think of all you could have done
At least you'll stay forever young
I guess you picked
The perfect way to die

ANOTHER REASON TO GET OUT THERE AND FIGHT

Ohh I guess you picked
The perfect way to die

New job, new city, new her
Bright eyed
You would have been proud if you knew her
Flashing lights in the mirror
Pull over
Pull over
A couple nights in detention and it's over
A whole life's over

They came marching in the city that day
They say
Carrying signs in the streets
Crying eyes in the streets
But they heard nothing from the city that day
They say
Just another one gone
And the city moved on
We're stuck here singing

Baby don't you close your eyes
'Cause this could be our final time
You know I'm horrible at saying goodbye
But I think of all you could have done
At least you'll stay forever young
I guess you picked
The perfect way to die
Ohh I guess you picked
The perfect way to die

Another dream lost
Another king and queen lost
Another broken promise
They refuse to make right
Ohh another night to live in fear
Ohh another night that you're not here
Another reason to get out there and fight

But I say
Baby don't you close your eyes
'Cause this could be our final time
You know I'm horrible at saying goodbye
But I think of all you could have done
At least you'll stay forever young
I guess you picked
The perfect way to die
Ohh I guess you picked
The perfect way...

Sit. Play.

ALI...

ALI SITS AT THE PIANO. ALI PLACES HER FINGERS ON THE KEYS, SITS UP STRAIGHT, TAKES A DEEP BREATH. ALI PRESSES DOWN ON THE KEYS.

BLACKOUT. END OF ACT ONE.

BABY DON'T YOU CLOSE YOUR EYES

'CAUSE THIS COULD BE OUR FINAL TIME

ACT TWO

HEARTBURN
LOVE LOOKS BETTER
WORK ON IT
AUTHORS OF FOREVER
FALLIN'
IF I AIN'T GOT YOU

ACT TWO

ACT TWO

PAWN IT ALL
LIKE YOU'LL NEVER SEE ME AGAIN
HALLELUJAH/LIKE WATER
NO ONE
EMPIRE STATE OF MIND

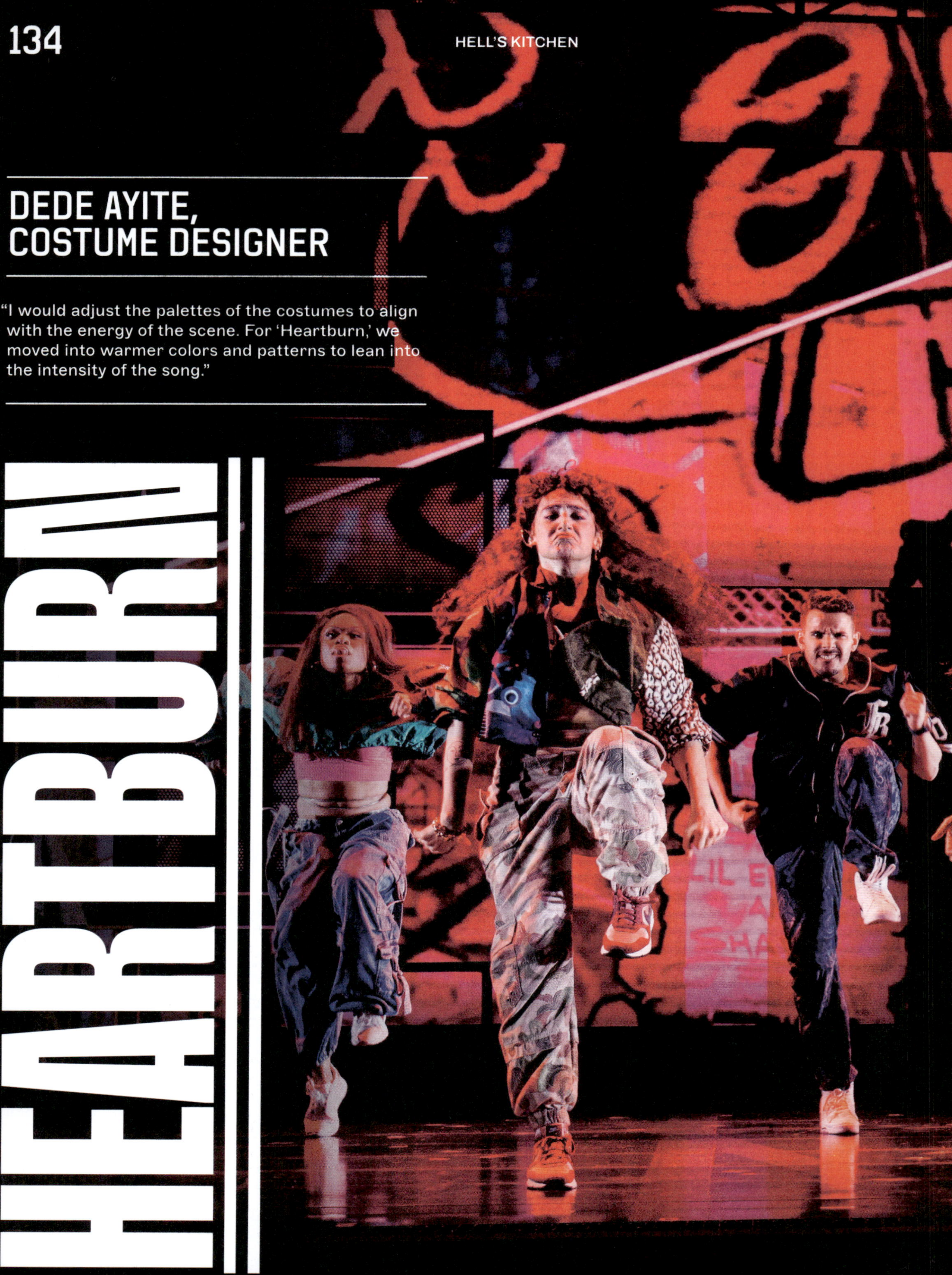

DEDE AYITE, COSTUME DESIGNER

"I would adjust the palettes of the costumes to align with the energy of the scene. For 'Heartburn,' we moved into warmer colors and patterns to lean into the intensity of the song."

HEARTBURN

IT'S LIKE I'M GOING INTO CARDIAC ARREST

ALI
It's been three weeks. I haven't heard from Knuck.
So my mother hasn't heard a word from me.

JERSEY
How long are we gonna do this?

ALI
Forever.

ENSEMBLE
Oh oh oh

JERSEY
Ali, I know you're mad at me.

ENSEMBLE
Oh oh oh

JERSEY
But we need to talk about it.

SONG: HEARTBURN

ENSEMBLE
Oh oh oh

JERSEY
Ali, we need to be able to have a conversation—

ENSEMBLE
Oh oh oh

ALI
Every time she tries to speak to me...

ENSEMBLE
Oh oh oh

ALI
I remember what she did to me...

ENSEMBLE
Oh oh oh

ALI
I remember what she did to Knuck.

ENSEMBLE
Oh oh oh

ALI
And something inside of me
Just, just...

ENSEMBLE
Oh oh oh

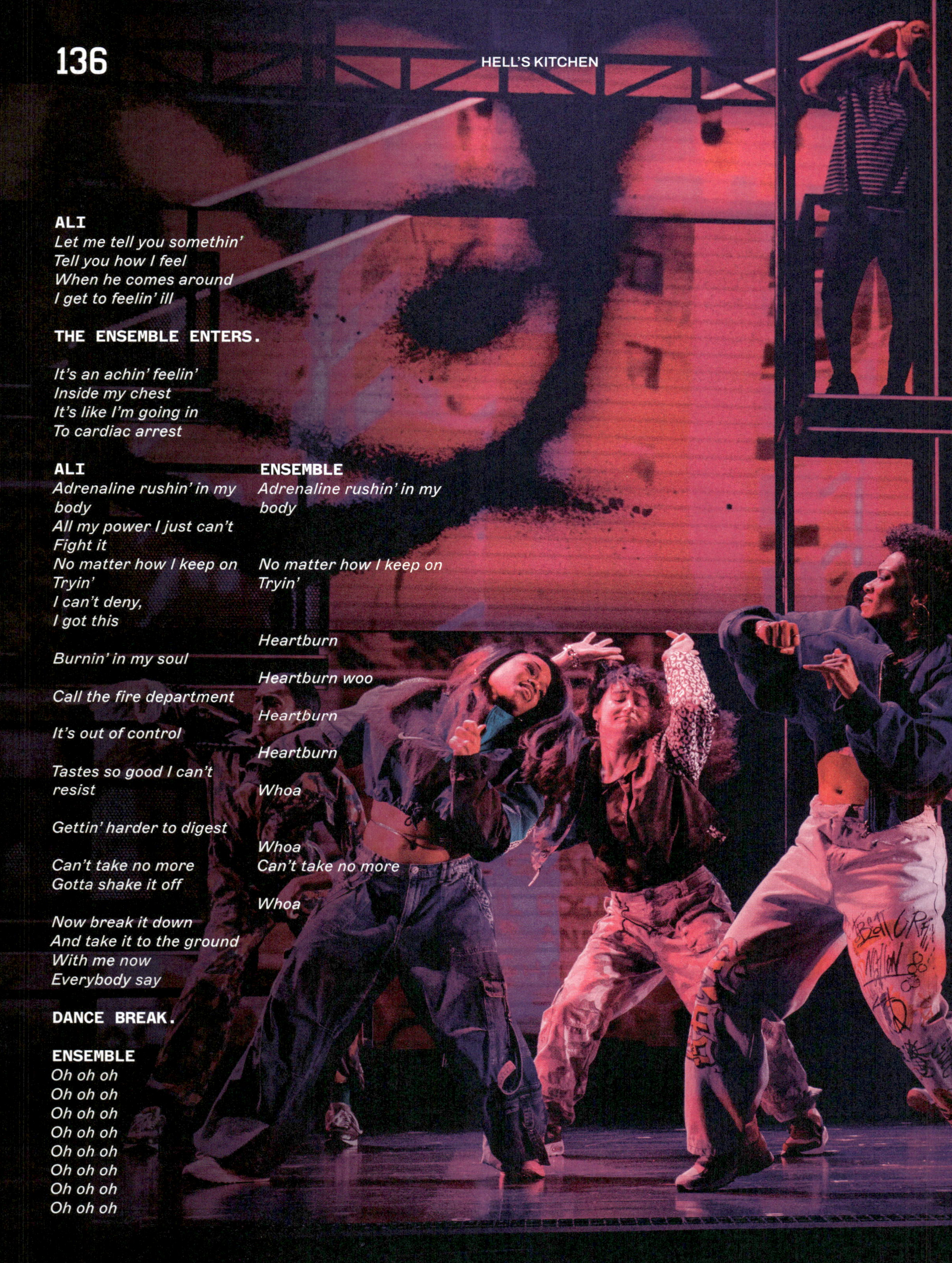

ALI
Let me tell you somethin'
Tell you how I feel
When he comes around
I get to feelin' ill

THE ENSEMBLE ENTERS.

It's an achin' feelin'
Inside my chest
It's like I'm going in
To cardiac arrest

ALI
Adrenaline rushin' in my body
All my power I just can't
Fight it
No matter how I keep on
Tryin'
I can't deny,
I got this

ENSEMBLE
Adrenaline rushin' in my body

No matter how I keep on
Tryin'

Heartburn

Burnin' in my soul

Heartburn woo

Call the fire department

Heartburn

It's out of control

Heartburn

Tastes so good I can't resist

Whoa

Gettin' harder to digest

Whoa

Can't take no more
Can't take no more
Gotta shake it off

Whoa

Now break it down
And take it to the ground
With me now
Everybody say

DANCE BREAK.

ENSEMBLE
Oh oh oh
Oh oh oh
Oh oh oh
Oh oh oh
Oh oh oh
Oh oh oh
Oh oh oh
Oh oh oh

ALI	**ENSEMBLE**
One, two, three, four	
Adrenaline rushin' in my body	*Adrenaline rushin' in my body*
All my power I just can't	
Fight it	
No matter how I keep on Tryin'	*No matter how I keep on Tryin'*
I can't deny,	
I got this	
	Heartburn
Burnin' in my soul	
	Heartburn woo
Call the fire department	
	Heartburn
It's out of control	
	Heartburn

ENSEMBLE
Shake it, shake it, shake it off
Go 'head girl
Shake it, shake it, shake it off
Ooooh
Shake it, shake it, shake it off
Go 'head girl
Shake it, shake it, shake it off
Ooooh

LOVE LOOKS BETTER

SHOSHANA BEAN, ACTOR (JERSEY)

"The majority of the songs for Jersey were already set when I came on board, but there were little things I had input on. I was really struggling with 'Love Looks Better,' so I asked if we could play with the tempo. They made it start off tender and then build to what it was, which felt more justified to me in the moment."

JERSEY I wasn't thinking about him. I was thinking about you. I'm always thinking about you. The only thing I'm ever thinking about is you.

SONG: LOVE LOOKS BETTER

All I, all I ever wanted
Was a dollar and a chance
Find, find what I'm made of, alright
Coming, coming from the bottom
Better learn how to dance
Find, find what you're made of, alright
Feel like my love is wasting every day,
Yeah
Get so damn tired of chasing every day,
Yeah
And now it's you I'm missing every day,
Yeah
Every day, yeah every day
So can we talk for a minute? Stop for a
Minute
All I wanna do is you
Oh can we touch for a second?
Be us for a second
Don't matter what I give it to

JERSEY	**ENSEMBLE**
My love looks better on you	*Ahh ahhh ahh*
My love looks better on you	*Ahh ahhh ahh*

ALI EXITS.

JERSEY
Promise you baby
Promise you baby
And now it's you I'm missing
Every day, yeah every day, yeah every day
So can we talk for a minute?
Just stop for a minute
All I wanna do is you
Oh can we touch for a second?
Be us for a second
Don't matter what I give it to
My love looks better on you

ENSEMBLE
Ahh ahhh ahh

JERSEY STOPS. LOOKS TO THE PHONE. PICKS IT UP. DIALS.

JERSEY Davis? I need help with our daughter.

(BEAT)

Just—just get here.

You're all I ever wanted
All I ever wanted
So can we talk for a minute?
Just stop for a minute
'Cause all I wanna do is you

WORK ON IT

NATASHA KATZ, LIGHTING DESIGNER

"'Work On It' is an anthem for all the complicated relationships in the show. The song is staged to give a feeling of working on a relationship, and Camille Brown's choreography beautifully tells the story of teenage love, bursting with adolescent hormones. I designed the lighting for this song as a comforting embrace of youth through warm light, isolating the dancing couple from the rest of the company. Then, as the number progresses, we slowly blend everyone together through light until the last moments, when color bursts through as a sign of hope for the future."

SONG: WORK ON IT

ENSEMBLE
Ha ha ha ha ha ha ha ha ha ha ha ha

KNUCK EXITS.

ALI	**ENSEMBLE**
He's not ready. He's been through a lot. I can wait. I can do whatever it takes to make this work. I can do whatever it takes to make us work.	*Ha ha ha ha ha ha* *ha ha ha ha ha ha* *Ha ha ha ha ha ha* *ha ha ha ha Ha ha* *Work on it work on it* *work on it baby*

ALI	**ENSEMBLE** (throughout)
Oh baby *Some may think that we moved too fast*	*Ha ha ha ha ha ha* *ha ha ha ha ha ha*

But I know you and you know me baby
That's what makes it last
Oh darling
So many lies were spread
About us
Oh, that's the heartache
That's the heartache that
Makes us build all the trust
I know some people like to say
That the easiest way
Is to fake it
We gonna make it
If we try
Gotta promise not to abuse it
If you use it
Don't lose it or break it
'Cause we gonna make it
You and I

ALI	**ENSEMBLE**
When they see us coming they gon' say	*Oh-oh oh-oh oh-oh oh-oh* *Oh-oh oh-oh oh-oh oh-oh* *Oh-oh oh-oh oh-oh oh-oh*
When they see us coming they gon' say	*Work on it work on it* *work on it baby* *Oh-oh oh-oh oh-oh oh-oh* *Oh-oh oh-oh oh-oh oh-oh* *Oh-oh oh-oh oh-oh oh-oh*
When they see us coming they gon' say	*Work on it work on it* *work on it baby*

AUTHORS OF FOREVER

SO LET'S CELEBRATE THE DREAMERS

VANESSA FERGUSON, ACTOR (TINY)

"Outside of those moments when I'm on stage, my favorite is Kecia Lewis singing 'Authors of Forever.' That low note she hits shakes the entire theater. It's normal to get applause from high notes, but for a woman to come out and sing like that, they have to applaud in the middle of the song. It's so uncommon."

SONG: AUTHORS OF FOREVER

MISS LIZA JANE
Where there's light
There must be a shadow
Cloudy skies
And rain make a rainbow
We are builders, we are breakers
We are givers, we are takers
And it's alright
We are seven billion stories
And we know the faith and glory
And it's alright

We are born on our own
And we die on our own
And we're here to make meaning of
What happens in between
We can hate
We can love
We can doubt
We can trust
But we're here to make meaning
For as long as we're breathing
And it's alright
And it's alright

MISS LIZA JANE Ali.
There will come a time when you have to do this—all this—on your own. My job is to prepare you to create your own future. Your job is to get ready to write your own story.

MISS LIZA JANE
We are lost and lonely people
And we're looking for a reason
And it's alright

WE EMBRACE THE SPACE BETWEEN US 'CAUSE IT'S ALRIGHT

ELLINGTON

So let's celebrate the dreamers
We embrace the space between us
'Cause it's alright

MISS LIZA JANE	**ENSEMBLE**
We're all in this boat	*Ahh*
Together	
And we're sailing toward	
the	
Future	
And it's alright	

MISS LIZA JANE AND ENSEMBLE
We can make the whole thing better
We're the authors of forever
And it's alright

ALI
We are

ALI, MISS LIZA JANE, AND ENSEMBLE
Born on our own
And we die on our own
And we're here to make meaning of
What happens in between
We could hate
We could love
We could doubt
We could trust
But we're here to make meaning
For as long as we're breathing

ENSEMBLE
And it's alright

MISS LIZA JANE
Whoever you are it's alright
Whoever you are it's alright
Wherever you are it's alright

'Cause if the drought hits tonight
Do not fear because you and I we are
Like water
Like water
Made to survive

MISS LIZA JANE	**ENSEMBLE**
And if the drought hits	*Aah*
Tonight	
Do not fear because you	*Aah*
and I	
We are	
Like water	
Like water	
Made to survive	*Made to survive*

TOM KITT, MUSIC CONSULTANT AND CO-ORCHESTRATOR

"You remember where you were when you first hear something that has an impact. And the first time I heard 'Fallin'' that was it. It was magical. So I never take it lightly, how lucky I am to be in this art form and to get to work alongside my heroes. I'm very lucky to be in this world of *Hell's Kitchen*."

FALLIN'

LOVIN' YOU DARLIN' MAKES ME SO CONFUSED

DAVIS You look good, Jersey Girl.

JERSEY Davis.

DAVIS No, I know. Never works, you and me. But Jersey Girl: I see you, you see me, and it all comes rushing back, the bad and the good.

SILENCE. ELECTRICITY. AND THEN…

SONG: FALLIN'

DAVIS
I keep on fallin'
In and out of love
With you

DAVIS SINGS A SONG OF SEDUCTION.

DAVIS
Sometimes I love ya
Sometimes you make me blue
Sometimes I feel good
At times I feel used
Lovin' you darlin'
Makes me so confused

I keep on fallin'
In and out of love with you
I never loved someone
The way that I love you

DAVIS	**JERSEY**
Oh, I never felt this way	
How do you give me so much	
Pleasure	*Pleasure*
And 'cause me so much pain	
	Ey ey
Just when I think	
	Just when I think
I've taken more than would a fool	*More than would a fool*
I start fallin' back in love	
With you	

DAVIS

I keep on fallin'
In and out of love with you
I never loved someone
The way that I love you
Fallin'
In and out of love with you
I never loved someone
The way that I love you

JERSEY AND DAVIS

Mmmm, mmmm
Mmmm, mmmm
Mmmm, mmmm
Mmmm, mmmm

JERSEY AND DAVIS	**ENSEMBLE**
Fall	
Fall	
Fall	*Fall*
Fall	*Fall*
Fall	*Fall*
Fallin'	*Fallin'*

JERSEY AND DAVIS

I keep on fallin'
In and out of love with you
I never loved someone
The way that I love you

I'm fallin'
In and out of love with you
I never loved someone
The way that I love you

I NEVER LOVED
SOMEONE THE WAY
THAT I LOVE YOU

LILY LING, MUSIC DIRECTOR

"I will never get sick of playing 'If I Ain't Got You.' It's a song I still remember hearing for the first time, I think in middle school or high school, over the radio. Playing with Brandon Victor Dixon is such a joy every night, because there's a consistency there, but there's also a sense of play. Without talking about it, wherever he goes, I'll go. It's one of the only songs in the show that's not clicked. There's no metronome, so you really are listening to each other, and when the band comes in, we drop in together, without click, without anything, we just feel it together. And we always drop at the same time. Even though we are rooms and floors apart, we still all feel it together, and that's an incredible experience every night, every single night. It's so much fun."

DAVIS You remember this song?

ALI No.

(to audience) I do. He knows I do.

DAVIS Oh. Well, I made up this song for you when you were a little girl.

ALI He knows as soon as he even brings this song up, it's ringing in my head, and I'm eight or I'm six or I'm four, and he's my dad, and I have no idea anything's ever going to be any different.

DAVIS You used to love it. And I used to love singing it to you. Bet I still will.

SONG: IF I AIN'T GOT YOU

DAVIS
Some people live for the fortune
Some people live just for the fame
Some people live for the power, yeah
Some people live just to play the game

Some people think that the physical things
Define what's within
And I've been there before, and that life's
A bore
So full of the superficial

Some people want it all
But I don't want nothing at all
If it ain't you baby
If I ain't got you baby
Some people want diamond rings
Some just want everything
But everything means nothing
If I ain't got you, yeah

Coming back to you?

ALI Oh... Pffft!

DAVIS Not even a little bit?
Alright, I'm gonna keep going.
Some people search for a
Damn, uh—

DAVIS PAUSES, LOOKS TO ALI TO PICK UP WHERE HE LEFT OFF.

ALI (spoken) Fountain.

DAVIS See? I knew you knew it.
That promises forever

ALI (spoken) Oh my god, young.

DAVIS
Young
Some people need

ALI
Three dozen roses

DAVIS
And that's the only way to
Prove you love them
Too late, I heard you, c'mon.

ALI
Hand me the world on a silver platter
And what good would it be

ALI AND DAVIS
With no one to share, with no one who truly
Cares for me

DAVIS
Some people want it all
But I don't want nothing at all
If it ain't you baby
If I ain't got you baby
Some people want diamond rings
Some just want everything
But everything means nothing
If I ain't got

ALI AND DAVIS
You
Some people want it all
But I don't want nothing at all
If it ain't you baby
If I ain't got you baby
Some people want diamond rings
Some just want everything
But everything means
Nothing

ALI
If I ain't got you, yeah

DAVIS	**ALI**
If I ain't got you with me	
Baby	
So nothing in this whole wide	*Whole wide*
World	*World*
Don't mean a thing	*Don't mean a thing*
	If I ain't got you with me
	Baby

BOTH ALI AND DAVIS ARE SITTING ON THE PIANO BENCH. ALI RESTS HER HEAD ON HIS SHOULDER.

ALI We sound good together.

DAVIS We do sound good together. We're going to have to do this again sometime.

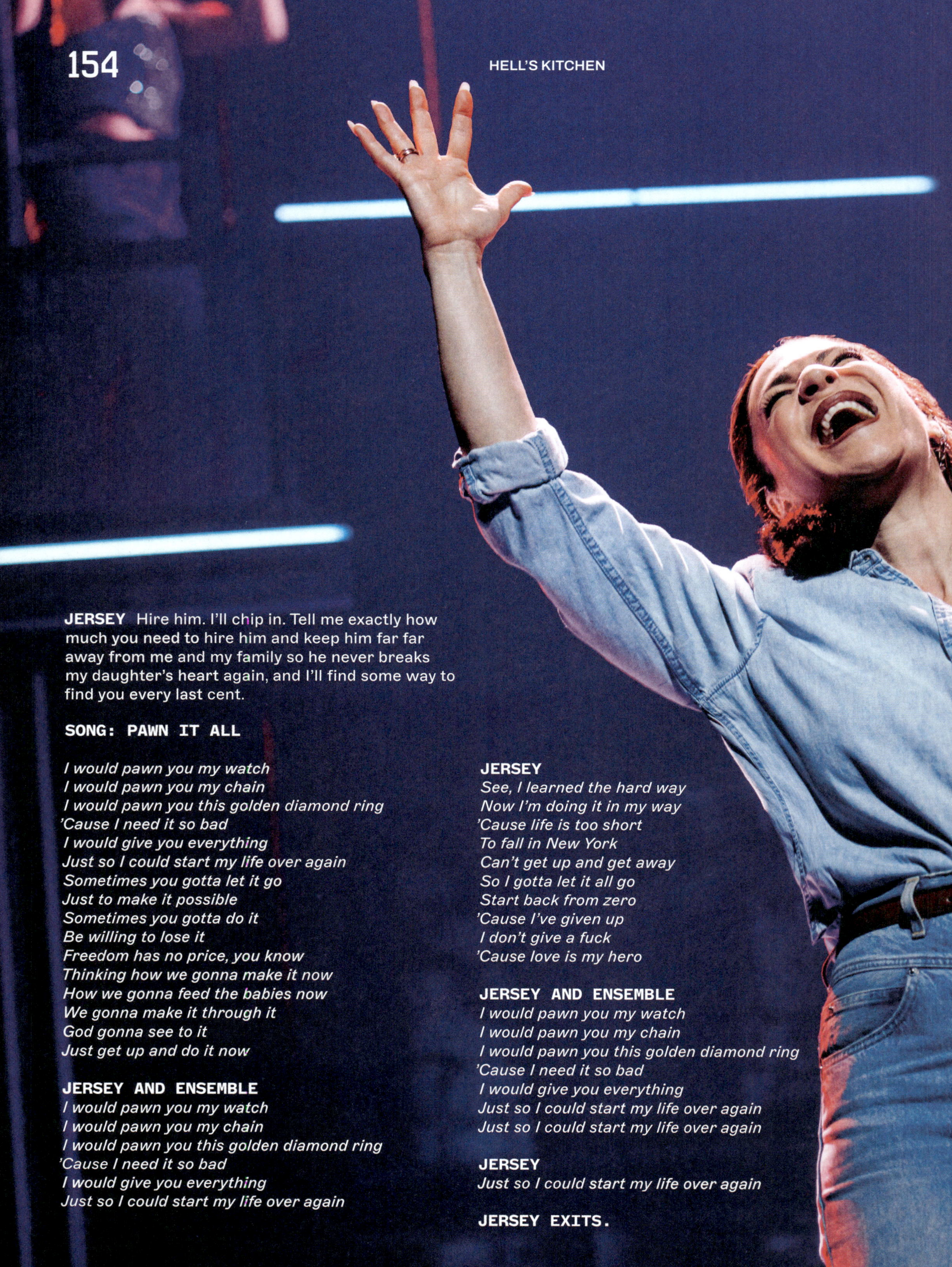

JERSEY Hire him. I'll chip in. Tell me exactly how much you need to hire him and keep him far far away from me and my family so he never breaks my daughter's heart again, and I'll find some way to find you every last cent.

SONG: PAWN IT ALL

I would pawn you my watch
I would pawn you my chain
I would pawn you this golden diamond ring
'Cause I need it so bad
I would give you everything
Just so I could start my life over again
Sometimes you gotta let it go
Just to make it possible
Sometimes you gotta do it
Be willing to lose it
Freedom has no price, you know
Thinking how we gonna make it now
How we gonna feed the babies now
We gonna make it through it
God gonna see to it
Just get up and do it now

JERSEY AND ENSEMBLE
I would pawn you my watch
I would pawn you my chain
I would pawn you this golden diamond ring
'Cause I need it so bad
I would give you everything
Just so I could start my life over again

JERSEY
See, I learned the hard way
Now I'm doing it in my way
'Cause life is too short
To fall in New York
Can't get up and get away
So I gotta let it all go
Start back from zero
'Cause I've given up
I don't give a fuck
'Cause love is my hero

JERSEY AND ENSEMBLE
I would pawn you my watch
I would pawn you my chain
I would pawn you this golden diamond ring
'Cause I need it so bad
I would give you everything
Just so I could start my life over again
Just so I could start my life over again

JERSEY
Just so I could start my life over again

JERSEY EXITS.

SHOSHANA BEAN, ACTOR (JERSEY)

"'Pawn It All' will always be one of the reasons I said yes, and one of the most exciting things I've ever gotten to do on a Broadway stage. One of my superpowers is my soul as a singer, and there isn't always a space for that in musical theater. Alicia wrote me a card right before we started previews. She wrote at the very end of it, 'Shine unhinged,' and I got that tattooed on my arm because it felt like the ultimate permission to be all of who you are, fearlessly, without limits, bravely, ferociously, to go past what you think you're capable of.

'Pawn It All' became my chance to speak fo not just every single mother, or any mother who has struggled to protect her child or struggled with the father of her child, but women in general, who have fought and have been doing it alone, and who have not been acknowledged, and who have tried to do i the right way, and just need to feel heard and seen."

PAWN IT ALL

SONG: LIKE YOU'LL NEVER SEE ME AGAIN

ALI I won't talk you out of leaving. I just want to listen. I just want to be here for you for as long as I can.

KNUCK
If I had no more time
No more time left to be here
Would you cherish what we had?

ALI
Was I everything

ALI AND KNUCK
That you were looking for?

ALI
If I couldn't feel your touch
And no longer were you with me
I'd be wishing you were here

ALI AND KNUCK
To be everything that I've been looking for

KNUCK
I don't want to forget the present is a
Gift

ALI
And I don't want to take for granted
The time you may have here with me

ALI AND KNUCK
'Cause lord only knows another day
Here's not really guaranteed

ALI	**KNUCK**
So every time you hold me	*Hold me*
Hold me like this is the last time	*Last time*
Every time you touch me	*Touch me*
Touch me like you'll never see me again	*Never see me again*
Every time you kiss me	*Kiss me*
Kiss me like this is the last time	*Last time*

THEY KISS.

KNUCK EXITS.

ALI
Oh oh oh

ALI AND KNUCK
Oh oh oh, oh oh oh
Oh oh oh, oh oh oh
Oh oh oh, oh oh oh

ALI
Was I everything that you were looking for?

ALICIA KEYS

"Here's another one that really travels far from its original inception. People think this is about someone singing to a lover. In truth, I wrote it about my grandmother when she was nearing the end of her days."

HALLELUJAH / LIKE WATER

DO NOT FEAR BECAUSE YOU AND I WE ARE LIKE WATER

CAMILLE A. BROWN, CHOREOGRAPHER

"I love the moment when David Guzman dances during Brandon's solo in 'Hallelujah/Like Water' at the top of the funeral scene, because to me, that's like an out-of-body experience that none of the other people see happening. It's almost like the dancer spirit is called to deliver the message through movement that Davis is giving at that time."

DAVIS I didn't know this Miss Liza Jane, but she sounds to me like the kind of woman that makes you want to be a better person. I don't know that I personally can become a better person. That ship might have sailed. But I do know a little bit about how to play the piano, and I'd like to do that in her honor if that's cool.

HE SITS AND BEGINS TO PLAY.

SONG: HALLELUJAH/LIKE WATER

And I don't know: maybe there's somebody out there who wants to say something but doesn't quite have the words. So I guess if there is anybody like that, she's welcome to come on up.

DAVIS PLAYS. ALI HESITATES.

Okay. I'll start.

There's a hole in my heart I've been hiding
I've been strong for so long that I'm blind
Is there a place I can go
Where the lonely river flows
Where fear ends and faith begins

ELLINGTON ROO

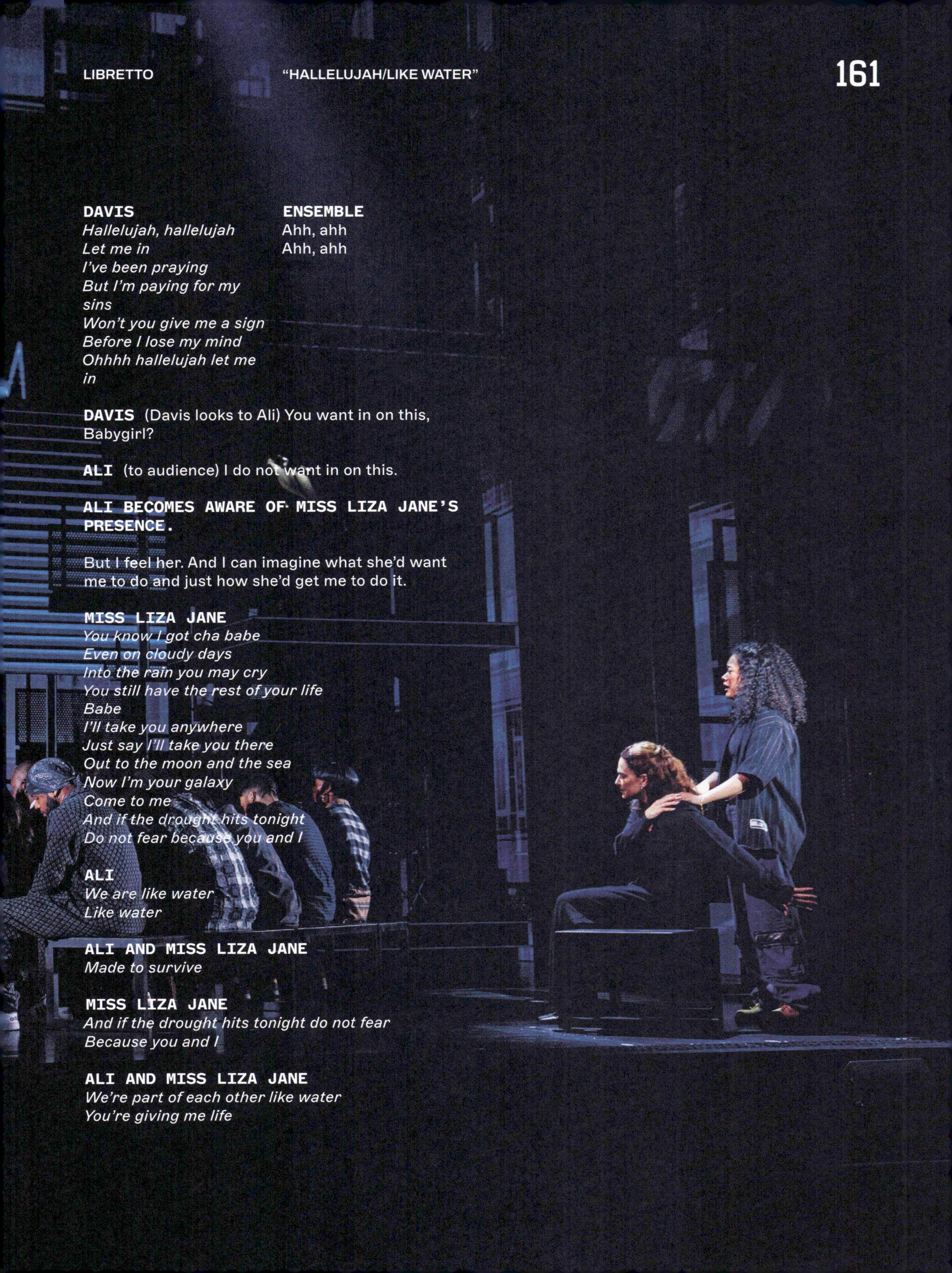

DAVIS	**ENSEMBLE**
Hallelujah, hallelujah	Ahh, ahh
Let me in	Ahh, ahh
I've been praying	
But I'm paying for my sins	
Won't you give me a sign	
Before I lose my mind	
Ohhhh hallelujah let me in	

DAVIS (Davis looks to Ali) You want in on this, Babygirl?

ALI (to audience) I do not want in on this.

ALI BECOMES AWARE OF MISS LIZA JANE'S PRESENCE.

But I feel her. And I can imagine what she'd want me to do and just how she'd get me to do it.

MISS LIZA JANE
You know I got cha babe
Even on cloudy days
Into the rain you may cry
You still have the rest of your life
Babe
I'll take you anywhere
Just say I'll take you there
Out to the moon and the sea
Now I'm your galaxy
Come to me
And if the drought hits tonight
Do not fear because you and I

ALI
We are like water
Like water

ALI AND MISS LIZA JANE
Made to survive

MISS LIZA JANE
And if the drought hits tonight do not fear
Because you and I

ALI AND MISS LIZA JANE
We're part of each other like water
You're giving me life

THE RESIDENTS (ENSEMBLE) RISE AND SING IN SUPPORT OF ALI.

ENSEMBLE
Ahh
Oh oh oh oohhh
Oh oh oh ohhh oh oh
Oh oh oh oohhh
Oh oh oh ohhh oh oh

ENSEMBLE
Oooooooo oooooo
hallelujah 2x

CRYSTAL
(adlib solo)

ALI AND DAVIS
Oooh ooooh

DAVIS
Please forgive me for my sins

ALI
Oooh hallelujah let me in

ENSEMBLE
Hmm

MISS LIZA JANE FADES INTO THE DARKNESS AS ALI TAKES OVER THE SONG, BACKED UP BY THE COMMUNITY.

ALI
And if the drought hits
Tonight
Do not fear because you and I
We are like water
Like water
Made to survive
And if the drought hits
Tonight
There's no fear because you
And I
We are part of each other
Like water
You've given me life

ENSEMBLE
Ahh
Ahh
Made to survive
Ahh

YOU AND ME
TOGETHER
THROUGH THE
DAYS AND
NIGHTS
NO ONE

KECIA LEWIS, ACTOR (MISS LIZA JANE)

"My absolute favorite moment, especially when we were in rehearsal and at the beginnings of our run Off-Broadway, was 'No One,' that moment between mother and daughter. I had a bit of a contentious relationship with my mother growing up. She loved me, but she couldn't conceive of someone who came from her having a career in the arts. She thought it was a hobby and something I would grow out of. Like Ali eventually figures out, I came to understand that was rooted in her love for me and her concern for me. That number every time would wreck me. I had to stop watching it because I would just be wrecked by it. And so that's probably my absolute favorite moment in the show."

JERSEY I'm sorry he's not here. I'm sorry Knuck's not here. I'm sorry—I am so sorry that Miss Liza Jane isn't here—

ALI Ma. You're here. You've always been here. Thank you.

SONG: NO ONE

JERSEY
I just want you close
Where you can stay forever
You can be sure
That it will only get better
You and me together
Through the days and nights
I don't worry 'cause
Everything's going to be alright
People keep talking
They can say what they like
But all I know is
Everything's going to be alright
No one, no one, no one
Can get in the way of what I'm feeling

ALI
No one, no one, no one
Can get in the way of what I feel for you,
You,

ALI AND JERSEY
You, you
Can get in the way of what I feel

ALI
When the rain is pouring down
And my heart is hurting
You will always be around
This I know for certain

JERSEY
You and me together
Through the days and nights
I don't worry 'cause

ALI AND JERSEY
Everything's going to be alright

ALI
People keep talking
They can say what they like
But all I know is

ALI AND JERSEY
Everything's going to be alright

ALI AND JERSEY
No one, no one, no one
Can get in the way of what I'm feeling
No one, no one, no one
Can get in the way of what I feel

JERSEY
I know

ALI
Some people search the world
To find

JERSEY
Something like what we have

ALI AND JERSEY
I know people will try
Try to divide something so real
So till the end of time I'm telling you
There ain't no one

ALI AND JERSEY
No one, no one, no one
Can get in the way of what I'm feeling
No one, no one, no one
Can get in the way of what I feel for you,

ENSEMBLE
No one, no one
Can get in the way, ohh
No one, no one
Can get in the way, ohh

ALI AND JERSEY
Oh, oh oh oh oh oh, oh oh oh oh oh, oh oh
Oh oh oh oh oh oh
Oh, oh oh oh oh oh, oh oh oh oh oh, oh oh
Oh oh oh oh oh oh

ENSEMBLE
(ALI AND JERSEY ADLIB RIFF OVER TOP)
Oh, oh oh oh oh oh, oh oh oh oh oh, oh oh
Oh oh oh oh oh oh
Oh, oh oh oh oh oh, oh oh oh oh oh, oh oh
Oh oh oh oh oh oh
Oh, oh oh oh oh oh, oh oh oh oh oh

ALI AND JERSEY
Can get in the way of what I feel for you

ALI AND JERSEY EMBRACE.

BLACKOUT.

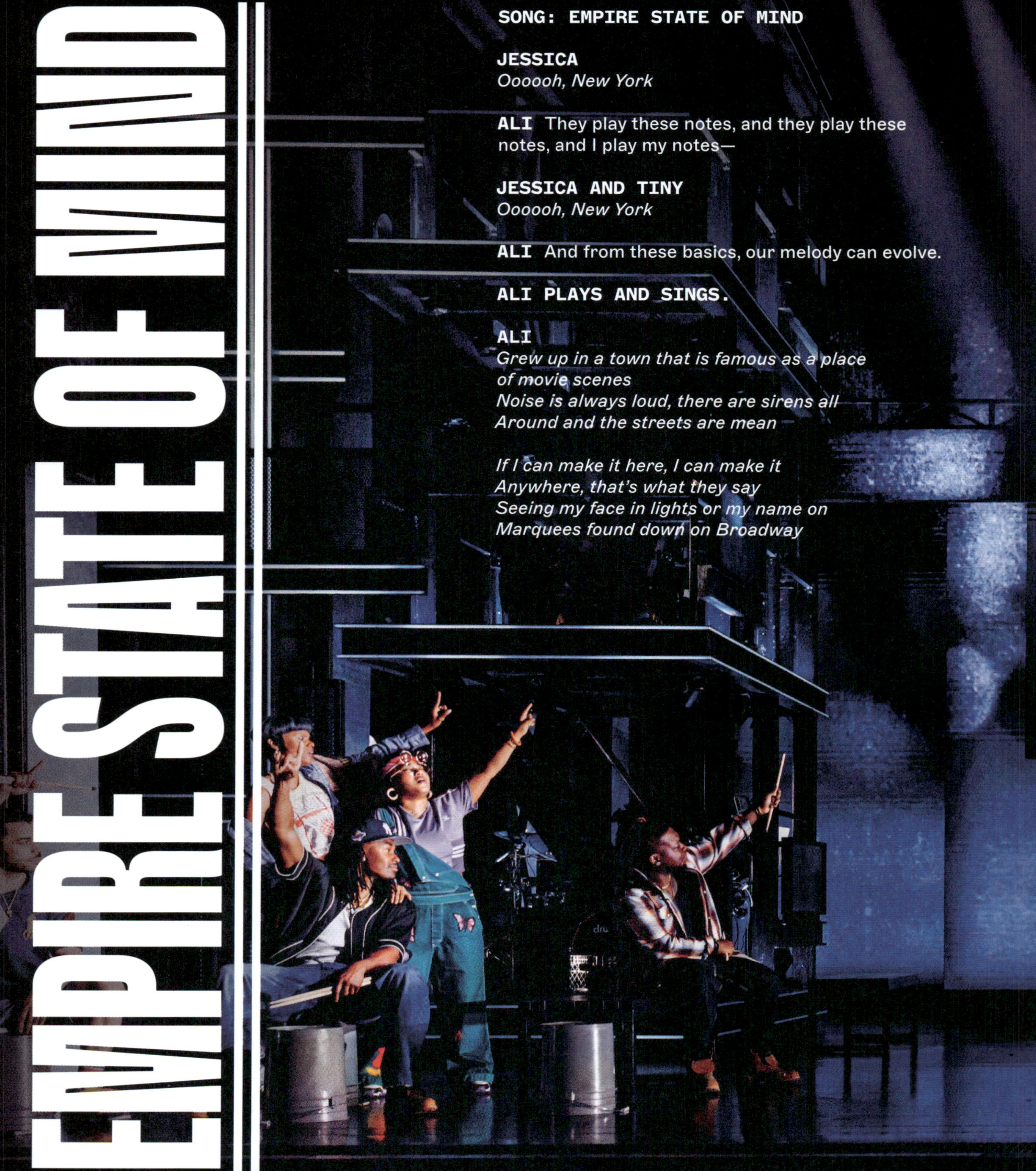

EMPIRE STATE OF MIND

SONG: EMPIRE STATE OF MIND

JESSICA
Oooooh, New York

ALI They play these notes, and they play these notes, and I play my notes—

JESSICA AND TINY
Oooooh, New York

ALI And from these basics, our melody can evolve.

ALI PLAYS AND SINGS.

ALI
Grew up in a town that is famous as a place
of movie scenes
Noise is always loud, there are sirens all
Around and the streets are mean

If I can make it here, I can make it
Anywhere, that's what they say
Seeing my face in lights or my name on
Marquees found down on Broadway

ADAM BLACKSTONE, MUSIC SUPERVISOR AND CO-ORCHESTRATOR

"I'm proud of how the song 'Empire' has transcended race, culture, age, creed. When you start hearing 'New York concrete...,' you can't help but get into it, no matter what. It's really cool to see, because I had only seen it before in a concert setting. To see it every night go up at the Shubert is a different thing. I think that's a testament to great songwriting. I think it's a testament to great book writing and where it lands in our show. The staging is incredible. The choreography from Camille A. Brown is incredible. And how Tom Kitt and I were able to collaborate, because that's the hip-hop record period, but we were able to bring it to the Broadway realm and stage in a way that makes me proud."

THESE STREETS WILL MAKE YOU FEEL BRAND NEW

ALI GETS UP AND JOINS THE COMMUNITY OUT IN FRONT OF THE BUILDING.

ALI	**JESSICA AND TINY**
Even if it ain't all it	
Seems, I got a pocketful of	
Dreams	
Baby I'm from New York!	
Concrete jungle where dreams	
Are made of	*Ahh*
There's nothing you can't do	
Now you're in New York!	
These streets will make you	
Feel brand new	*Ahh*
Big lights will inspire you	*Ahh*
Hear it for	
New York	*New York*
New York, New Yooork!	*New York, New Yooork!*

KNUCK DRUMS.

AND OVER THE COURSE OF THE SONG, EVERYONE JOINS IN: ALI SINGING, JESSICA AND TINY ON BACKUP, 'RIQ AND Q RHYMING, THE WHOLE CITY ON HARMONY.

ALI
On the avenue, there ain't never a curfew,
Ladies work so hard

ALI AND TINY
Such a melting pot, on the corner selling
Rock, preachers pray to God

JESSICA	**ALI AND TINY**
Hail a gypsy cab, takes me	
Down from Harlem to	
the Brooklyn Bridge	*Bridge*

'RIQ AND Q
Someone sleeps tonight with a hunger far
More than an empty fridge

KNUCK
I'mma make it by any means, I got a

ALI AND KNUCK
Pocketful of dreams

ALI	**ENSEMBLE**
I'm from New York!	*New York*

ALI
Concrete jungle where dreams are made of

JERSEY	
There's nothing you can't do	**ENSEMBLE**
Now you're in New York!	*New York*

DAVIS
These streets will
Make you feel
Brand new

JERSEY
Big lights will inspire you

ALI AND KNUCK	**ENSEMBLE**
Talking bout New York	*New York*

AND SOMEWHERE IN HERE, JERSEY ENTERS, WATCHES HER DAUGHTER WITH GREAT PRIDE.

ALI AND KNUCK	**ENSEMBLE**
Concrete jungle where	
Dreams are	
Made of	*Ahh*
There's nothing you can't do	*Ahh*
Now you're in New York!	*New York*

ALI AND KNUCK	**ENSEMBLE**
These streets will	
Make you feel	
Brand new	*Ahh*
Big lights will	
Inspire you	*Ahh*
Hear it for	
New York,	*New York,*
New York, New Yooork!	*New York, New Yooork!*

ALI AND ENSEMBLE
One hand in the air for the big city
Street lights, big dreams, all looking pretty
No place in the world that can compare
Put your lighters in the air, everybody say
Yeah! Yeah! Yeah! Yeah!
In New York!
Concrete jungle where dreams are made of
There's nothing you can't do
Now you're in New York!

AND SOMEWHERE IN HERE, MISS LIZA JANE ENTERS AND SHOWS ALI SOME LOVE.

MISS LIZA JANE	**ENSEMBLE**
These streets will make you	
Feel brand new	*Ahh*
Big lights will inspire you	*Ahh*

ALI AND ENSEMBLE
Hear it for New York
New York
New York!

ENSEMBLE
New York
New York
New York!

ALI AND ENSEMBLE
She be spiked out
She could trip a referee
Ay ay ay
Tell by her attitude
That she most definitely from
From from

Statue of Liberty
Long live the World Trade
Ay ay ay

Long live the queen yo
She from the Empire State that's
That's
That's
That's
New York
New York
New York!

CURTAIN.

END OF SHOW.

4

COSTUMES & DANCE

This page: Maleah Joi Moon backstage, showing off her FUBU jersey
Previous page: Maleah Joi Moon as Ali performing "Empire State of Mind"

LOCKING DOWN AN AESTHETIC

By spring of 2023, readings and workshops had shaped *Hell's Kitchen* into something the team felt was audience-ready, and the Public had reserved space in the largest of its five theaters for the show. A month-long run would premiere in October (which would be extended by another five weeks due to audience demand). It was time to focus on key visual elements for the company: aesthetics and movement.

Costume designer Dede Ayite's Broadway credits include *A Soldier's Play*, *Slave Play*, *American Son*, and *Children of a Lesser God*. Michael Greif was already working with her on *Days of Wine and Roses* when *Hell's Kitchen* was ready to start figuring out its look, and he called on her again.

Michael Greif, director
When *Hell's Kitchen* started becoming a real thing, it was easy to be excited about proposing Dede Ayite as the costume designer. She grew up in Ghana, so she wasn't here in '90s New York, but she has a great way of being both in the culture and being an observer. It was a lot of research for her, but also an awful lot of *This feels right for the people that I know*.

Alicia Keys
Just as important as it was for Kris to understand the energy of New York in order to write *Hell's Kitchen*, so it was for every single person who was part of creating how it was visually expressed. For this show, it's more clothing than costumes. I love the reality of the look Dede put together, and I would wear those looks today. She was capturing New York City and that vibrancy, that style—and yet also making it timeless. She pushed the boundaries farther than just capturing the moment.

Dede Ayite, costume designer
The '90s were a fantastic time, a bold and energetic time. That younger generation coming up wanted to be seen. Their expression of self was through the cut of their clothes and the layering of different textures. The exciting thing about what I get to do as a costume designer is find ways in which clothing can speak to the psychology of an individual or a people, and it can also identify the reaction of individuals to their moment. The heart of this piece is cemented in the '90s, however, it's also in conversation with New York City today.

Alicia Keys
Dede definitely pushed the boundaries when it came to the dancers' costumes in "Kaleidoscope." That moment is like a waking dream; Ali's seeing all these things come to life that she's never seen before, and Dede wanted to express that through the clothing. I was skeptical about this at first, because I didn't want things to seem fantastic. I wanted it to be real. But when Dede showed her vision, and it came to life, and I saw the way the colors and the brightness illuminated the dreamlike state, it was absolutely right.

Another part of the costume story that's kind of funny is when we show Davis and Jersey in the '70s.

Costume designer Dede Ayite sprinkled '90s labels throughout the show, featuring Black designers whose clothes were popularized by hip-hop artists. She found a vintage FUBU (For Us By Us) jersey for Ali, then collaborated with the label to produce a special edition, adjusting the intensity of the orange to make sure it worked well for the stage.

I was very against doing this. I didn't want them to revert back to another era. I was like, "We don't need it. I don't want to." I fought Michael so hard on doing this '70s moment, but he felt like bringing people into the past would show the passage of time.

I didn't want the schtick. But when Dede pulled together these looks from the '70s it became quite fun, and it did allow us to travel with Jersey and Ali, as Jersey was connecting with Ali by telling her about the past, and as we're developing their relationship for the viewer. It was good to see Jersey and Davis in that time and then fast-forward back to today. Once again, Michael was right. I fought him on a lot of things he ended up being right on. That was one of them. But I love how everything Dede did was always based in the real. The way we pulled mood boards and talked through how it should feel and look was always based on being organic and true.

Dede Ayite
My joy is to identify what pieces will allow me to highlight a person's body in a way that feels flattering and feels like them. In *Hell's Kitchen*, I got to play around with so many different shapes and silhouettes, patterns and colors, and I got to dress a variety of bodies, skin tones, and cultures.

Michael Greif
I think our company was a huge delight for Dede. Being able to tell a full story with the ensemble allowed her to paint a landscape.

Dede Ayite
I definitely think of the show as a painting, and then I break it down into smaller paintings, so each scene has its own energy and color palette. Then I further break that down into each character, how the pieces might move in the show, and how the performers need to do what they need to do, especially in terms of dancing. Michael also thinks of shape and space, so it was fun to work together in shaping the space through colors and silhouettes.

Dede shaped the look of Ali and her friends by turning to the trends and designers of their time, often looks that were identified with pop culture icons. In the "Work On It" duet, dancer Reid Clarke wears a yellow outfit that is a nod to Aaliyah, the late rap

In "Work On It," featured dancer Reid Clarke wears a two-piece set that is a reference to the late singer Aaliyah, who wore a similar yellow outfit. "It's a bit of a nod to those in the know," says Dede.

artist who helped popularize street style. In "The Gospel," an ensemble member wears a shirt from Coogi, the Australian brand that Biggie Smalls referenced in more than one of his songs. Also on trend are Timberlands or "Butters," the waterproof leather work boot, and Tommy Hilfiger boxer shorts, which peek out above the waistbands of jeans.

Dede Ayite
I have to say, I'm most excited and proud of what Ali wears at the top of the show. We were able to find this vintage FUBU jersey that is, for me, iconic. FUBU stands for "for us by us," and the brand was started by four Black men from Queens. It felt important to foreground that. Right off the bat, Ali is letting you know she's present, she's here, she's a Black woman trying to find her way in the world, and you're going to go on the journey with her. Featuring FUBU was a way to celebrate designers who were able to take a stance and say, "We're here to celebrate us." That's important.

As a Black woman who was born and raised in Ghana, I'm very fortunate to have grown up where the majority of the people look like me. I often think about how it is for those who grow up in a space where, every day, there's imagery that tells you you're not enough. That is additional labor that you have to navigate. I don't think people understand the weight of that labor, what it's like to go through the world and everywhere you turn, the message is that you need straighter hair or lighter skin or European features. In thinking of the weight of that labor, I felt it was important to create a space in which Blackness and individuality could be celebrated, which then allows, I'm hoping, for all cultures to be celebrated.

DRAMATURGY IN MOTION

Choreographer Camille A. Brown's Broadway debut was in 2012 with *A Streetcar Named Desire*, followed by the Tony Award–winning *Once on This Island*. But the Jamaica, Queens, native has been active in the dance world for more than two decades and heads her own company, Camille A. Brown & Dancers (CABD). Her distinct approach pulls from traditional genres such as modern, tap, and ballet, and from social dance styles that mark a point in time, which for this show would include the Running Man, the Bogle, and the Wop.

COSTUMING THE '90S

When Dede Ayite saw her first *Hell's Kitchen* rehearsal, the energy of it blew her away. "It captured the heart and intensity of New York City," she says, and her mission was to support that through costumes. "Here's a younger generation coming up that wants to be seen, and so their expression of self is through the cut and layering of their clothes." For Dede, the hip-hop styles Ali and her friends adopt articulate resistance, Black culture, and Black love.

In their research, Dede and her team did deep dives into the magazines and music videos of the 1990s. They scoured vintage stores and auction sites, incorporating looks from Coogi, Pelle Pelle, and Tommy Hilfiger. Timberland boots were non-negotiable. Still, the costumes needed to be more than baggy silhouettes and popular name brands. Dede wanted to show that the teenagers were not only dressing to be different from the generation before them (exhibit A: Ali's mother often appears in high-waisted, form-fitting jeans), but they were also using clothes to claim identities.

The overall vibe of Dede's costumes washes over audiences as soon as the cast takes the stage in the show's big opening number, "The Gospel." But the full impact is realized gradually, in her incredibly specific attention to detail and attention to the individuals underneath the costumes.

Chloe's Painted Shoes and Pants

In "Gospel" and "Empire," dancer Chloe Davis wears embellished camo pants and sneakers. Dede asked legendary theatrical dyer and distresser Hochi Asiatico to paint gold highlights and splashes of white on the pants—to embody Chloe's dynamic movement—and to extend the orange and green camo pattern onto the shoes. "As much as my work is about the look of the show and the character I'm shaping," Dede says, "it's also about celebrating the performer within that track." After spending time with Chloe, Dede asked Hochi to embellish the shoes with a deconstructed crown and the word "Queen," both rendered in a graffiti style. "I think of Chloe as a queen," Dede says. "She's strong, she's beautiful, she's multifaceted."

Niki Saludez's Blue Sky Coveralls

These coveralls are worn by dancer Niki Saludez in "Kaleidoscope." Dede wanted to underscore that scene as a moment of liftoff for Ali, and she does it here with Hochi Asiatico's handpainted images of open skies and the breaking of chains. Dede also used a quote from the writer and activist Audre Lorde: "In our world, divide and conquer must become define and empower." Those lines appear on the back of the

Chloe Davis's painted sneakers and pants

A costume fellow working on Niki Saludez's coveralls

Tiny
Tiny
Love

garment, screen printed using Alicia Keys's own handwriting and surrounded by glittering wing appliques. "I thought of the dancers as having many of their own liftoffs," says Dede. "It's important for me to consider the performer and how to marry the movement in the scene to the dancers themselves."

Tiny's Shirt

The plaid fabrics pieced together in Tiny's oversized button-down shirt signify the character's tomboy nature. They're primarily blue and brown, traditionally masculine colors, but they're also patchworked, which provides a note of softness. Dede again brought in Hochi Asiatico to put Tiny's stamp on the piece. He painted on her name in graffiti style, complete with paint drips and a brick wall background. On top of that, he superimposed images of the gold bamboo hoop earrings that were popular at the time, customized here with Tiny's name and the word "love." "It felt like a unique way to say, 'I'm here, look at me, I'm present,'" Dede says. "There's a strength in being able to say, 'My name is XYZ.' Especially when you think about Black history and Black ancestors, holding onto an identity is important."

Ali's Empire Jacket

It took many hands to execute the masterpiece of a jacket Ali wears in the final "Empire" scene. The garment Dede designed, a dark denim woven through with shimmering Lurex threads, was built by Jimmy McBride, who incorporated individually sewn strips of fabric into elaborate basketweave sleeves that suggest how Ali's life is woven together. Costume illustrator Bee Gable worked with Dede to create and proportion a recognizable New York skyline to fit on the jacket back. A final collaboration was with Eric Winterling's costume studio, which specializes in the rhinestone work that appears all over the jacket—as a geometric pattern, in the fully encrusted graffiti-style initial *A*, and as a painterly element in depicting the skyline. "In the same way that I've used paint to shape some garments and give them their unique qualities," Dede says, "here I'm using rhinestones to capture the sun starting to rise for Ali."

Meleah Joi Moon getting their hair and makeup done

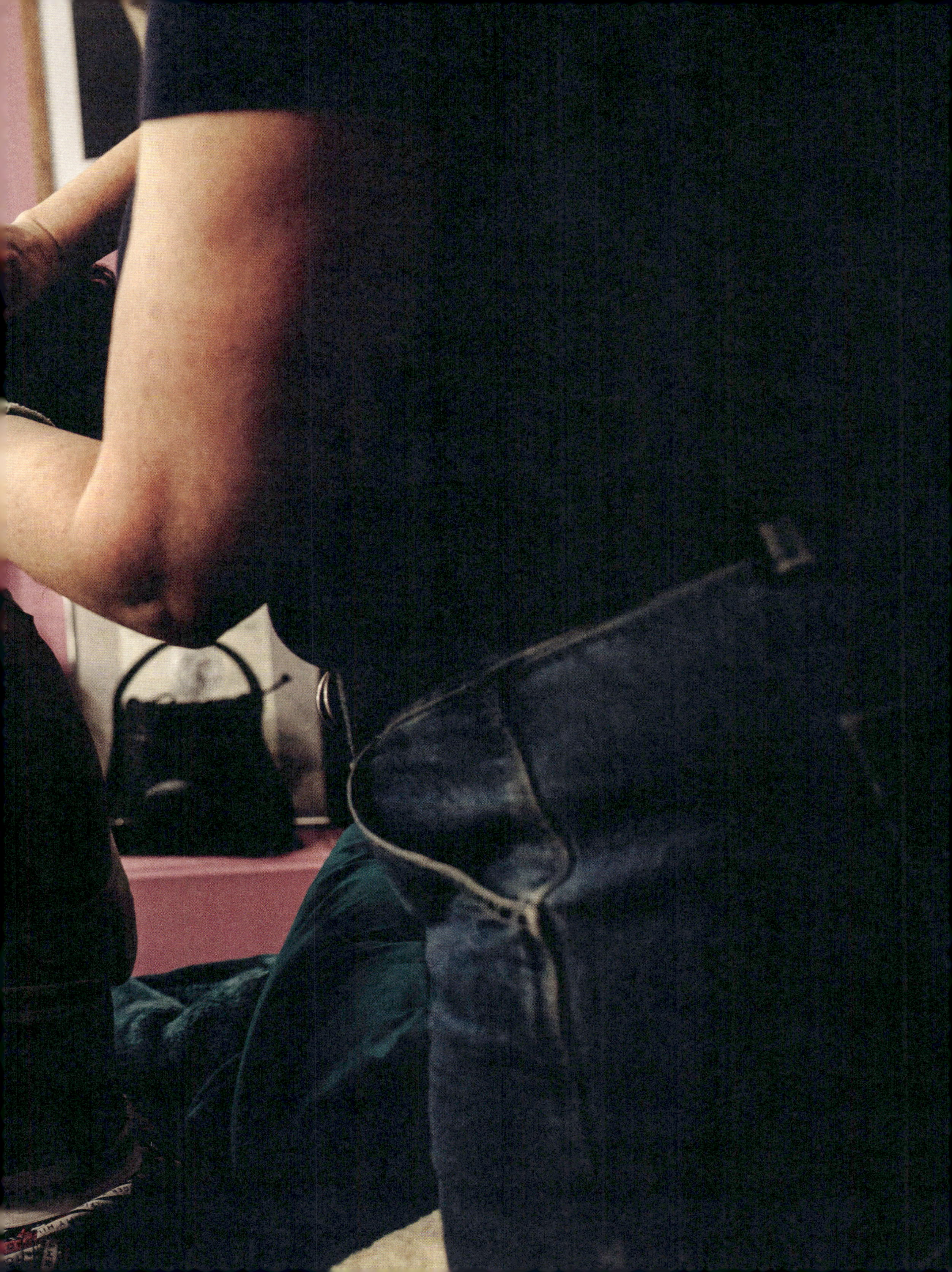

Camille A. Brown

Michael Greif
I rarely have the opportunity to have a dance ensemble in one of my shows. Honestly, it happened once in my career, and it didn't go well, and maybe that's why I've avoided it. But with this, I thought a dance ensemble would be amazing. Because I knew I was bringing a great project to the Public, I was in a good position to say, "Here are some conditions: I think there's a dance ensemble." The Public said, "We agree." It was a joy to know that I could say to any choreographer, "Guess what? You have your pick of people, and they don't have fifteen other things to do."

Aaron Lustbader, executive producer
It's very unusual that a show has eight dancers who just dance. Broadway shows are generally made up of triple threats. You can act, you can sing, you can dance—maybe not so much on the acting for strong dancers, but they sing. There's an economy to having all of that in combination and thankfully, I wasn't involved in the show at this stage, because I probably would have argued arduously against the idea of having eight bodies onstage who just dance. And yet it's so fundamental to the success of the show that this group of talented performers exists.

Mandy Hackett, co-producer
When Michael said to me, "Camille [the choreographer] is going to need real dancers," it was relatively early in terms of putting together the production, so the budget was still in flux. If it had been ten months later, it would have been a whole drama. But I knew if we were going to hire Camille, we needed to support her. Camille is one of the truest artists. That's one of the things about *Hell's Kitchen* that I think is so true to its success. There's no ego. It is artists at the pinnacle of their artistic journey.

Michael Greif
I always feel that you need to get the story right before bringing in a choreographer. But everybody loves when you start staging numbers, and in our case, there was a fantastic step up into reality when Camille started putting numbers on their feet. The show became more active and vivid, and a lot of things fell into place, including how are we going to get away with these quiet, little two-person scenes? Well, now we knew we could, because they were next to big, vibrant musical events. You gain confidence and start to understand the rhythm of the piece.

Mandy Hackett
Michael and I were both excited to introduce Alicia to Camille Brown, who I had worked with a bunch of times. Alicia looked at some tape of Camille and read about her, and said, "Okay, let's go with her." I texted Camille, "Do you have some time to talk?" We talked, and I told her about the project. There was silence on the other end of the phone. Then she said, "Mandy, this is my dream come true. I worship Alicia Keys."

Alicia Keys
I believe that this show could be done with one piano and one light, but we did also need this sense of space and time, and what Camille choreographs brings that in a way that is truly unlike anything I've experienced. I was moved beyond words when I first saw the way she choreographed to the music, because it was another character. She brought what I never even thought we needed.

Michael Greif
There is an exuberance that distinguishes Camille's work. It flips easily back and forth between community members who are actual human beings, dancing in Ali's world, and those dancers being extensions of Ali's emotional state or her imaginings.

"Camille has done with hip-hop and street dance exactly what Jerome Robbins did with ballet in West Side Story."

Oskar Eustis, artistic director, Public Theater
I confess I have a dog in this fight, because I'm on Camille's advisory board for her dance company, and the Public supported her first directing job with *for colored girls who have considered suicide / when the rainbow is enuf*. I'm a total fanboy.

Camille has done with hip-hop and street dance exactly what Jerome Robbins did with ballet in *West Side Story*. He took ballet, translated it into the musical theater, and put it on very unlikely bodies. And by doing that, he ennobled the street kids, basically saying these kids are worthy of being seen as larger-than-life heroes and heroines. Camille is doing the same thing with the dance vocabulary of hip-hop. She's elevating it to a rigorous classical form and saying this dance and the people who made up this dance are worthy of the kind of precision and virtuosity that we associate with the most exalted forms of movement. It's got the formal discipline of the ballet and modern dance that Camille's trained in, infused with the street dance that is diegetic to the neighborhood of Hell's Kitchen and to the world that Ali grew up in. As a result, it doesn't feel like a pop superstar has been watered down to make a musical theater piece, because the dance and the movement are at the level of that music.

Camille A. Brown, choreographer
There is no one way of being a New Yorker. Someone from Queens is very different from someone from the Bronx. It wasn't about creating New York as a monolith. We wanted the choreography to feel gritty and to feel real. That comes from the body understanding who they are and where they are in the moment. Some of the dancers weren't even born in this time period, so it was also about asking people to do their research. Every day before rehearsal, one of the dancers could

Jackie Leon, Vanessa Ferguson, and Maleah Joi Moon during rehearsal

HAIR INSPO

MIA NEAL, HAIR DESIGNER

This was a fun show for me to do because it's the first time I've ever done the '90s era, and that's when I grew up. I come from Gary, Indiana, right outside Chicago, and hair is a huge deal there. I started doing hair in my aunt's salon. I was just a shampoo girl, but if you showed up late, then I became your hair stylist as a punishment. A lot of the clients were older, in their '60s and '70s, but I didn't care. You were going to get finger waves with rods, even if you did not wear your hair like that. These were businesswomen who wore their hair pressed up, but not if you ended up in my chair. That was when I was in high school, and we were trying our hardest to be New York. We were duplicating everything we saw in *Vibe* magazine and in *The Source*. Whatever I saw a popular artist doing, that's what I needed to do.

Everybody goes through a struggle with their hair. But in particular when you're biracial, and not in a household where your parent has the same texture as you, you definitely have your own journey of trying to figure out, *What do I actually like, and how do I achieve that?* So we see Ali with a ponytail first, where it's a lot of hair and she just wants to get it out of her face. She hasn't quite figured out what to do with those curls. And then she loses the ponytail when she starts to engage with this guy, because now she's trying to find a more mature look. In the second act, she still pins the front to get it out of her face, but she's wearing her hair down.

JERSEY

Alicia shared photos of her mom during that time period, and her hair was big and curly and red. I needed to pull from that, but at the same time make sure it looked good on Shoshana Bean. You can't always duplicate a style exactly, because body types are different, neck and shoulder ratios are different, and it would be easy to swallow up Shoshana in big hair. So we found a reddish-brown color and a style that was soft, but pulled off of her face.

MISS LIZA JANE

Her hair tells the story of her getting sicker. She starts off with it down, and then it slowly starts to get wrapped up, and then she ends up with the entire thing covered, to show that she might be losing her hair. She also just isn't in a place where she can take care of it anymore, so we watch it slowly disappear underneath these head wraps.

TINY

Tiny's look is T-Boz from TLC. She had these long sideburns, and a bowl cut that went around and was short in the back. It screams '90s.

JESSICA

There was a hip-hop artist named Lady of Rage back then who rhymed, "I rock rough and stuff with my Afro Puffs." She brought these Afro puffs back. For Jackie Leon, I ended up twisting the front back, because that was also popular and it complemented the actress's face.

The cast rehearsing “The Gospel”

choose three songs for our warmup, and the only requirement was that they were from the '90s. No one knew in advance what each person had selected, so it was a "name that tune" kind of thing. That was also great for community building, which is an integral part of making a space authentic.

Camille's ensemble is a mix of dancers she's worked with for years and dancers who came to the show through the audition process. For several of them, it was their Broadway debut.

Kate Murray, casting director

The dance auditions were unique to anything I've worked on in that dancers were required to bring who they were to the steps. It wasn't enough for Camille and her team that you do the steps perfectly. You had to invest yourself in the choreography. When dancers were about to present the choreo that they'd learned, Camille and her team would ask their names and where they were from. And then Camille would say, "Show us. Show us how Buffalo shows up in what you do. Show us Fredericksburg." And everyone who was not dancing had to vocally cheer them on.

Camille was adamant that any social dances she incorporated would do more than mark the time period. They had to help tell the story, and they had to tell it in Camille's voice.

Camille A. Brown

One challenge was, how do you contribute to songs that have clearly already succeeded? How do you provide movement through storytelling that gives people all the feels they originally had listening to the song, but then also presents new ideas?

I describe what I do as a jambalaya, because it's not just one thing. It's involving many things and influences. But one thing that I wanted to make sure of was that my voice came before my influences, because we're all influenced by a lot of things, but it's important for me to make sure that my voice is at the forefront. It's like how you knew when Ella Fitzgerald was singing, you knew when Whitney Houston was singing, you know when Alicia Keys is singing. Their voices are very distinct.

Michael Greif

I asked Camille to dress up "Gramercy Park" because it has these long choruses where everyone is going "mm-mm-mm-mm," and I knew I would run out of silent material for Knuck and Ali. So Camille brought this group of men into the number, and after I watched it the first time, I said, "Oh, I think you're onto something amazing." Of the original four dancers, one was

"She captured all of that without saying one word and completely through the movement...It's my favorite choreography in Hell's Kitchen"

a Black man, and we made sure that he was always the first man that Knuck saw. Knuck's identification with that man has taken on enormous meaning in the musical; it's a beautiful physical representation of everything he's singing about: being misunderstood, trying to satisfy other people's perceptions of himself, and sometimes making the mistakes that fall into those perceptions.

Camille A. Brown
I spoke a lot with Chris Lee and the dancers, who were all people of color, about what it means to exist as a male-identifying person of color in America. We talked about the story of Knuck trying to push through those stereotypes that are often placed on people of color. My process is also about conversations, because I'm interested in their choice as a dancer. I'm interested in understanding what informed the choice, and a lot of times their experiences inform what we'll do.

Mandy Hackett
Flash forward, Camille did a workshop where we staged three or four numbers. It felt like watching New York. It felt like watching something so now, so fresh, so contemporary. Alicia was so happy. Terri was so happy. We were all pinching ourselves and each other.

Alicia Keys
I'll never forget the first time that I saw "Gramercy Park." We restructured that song and even rewrote some lines to capture the feelings Knuck was having. The song fit beautifully into that moment, but then when Camille put the dancers inside of it and started to choreograph, you felt the depth of this story. You could see these four different men try so hard to not be the stereotype that everybody assumes they are. You witness this through the dance. You also experience the anger, the anger that comes with wearing this mask, and the frustration and the desire to be freed from this cage. She captured all of that without saying one word and completely through the movement. She took what I already knew was a special scene and made it so much more. It's my favorite choreography in *Hell's Kitchen*.

Oskar Eustis
"Kaleidoscope" makes me crazy. That is the moment where we see Ali become an artist in her head. To me, that's where Camille's work first lifts off, and you realize, *Oh God, this is something special*. Her choreography is doing something dramaturgically that choreography normally doesn't do. It is becoming the embodiment of Ali's artistry, of her spirit.

Camille A. Brown
"The Gospel" used a lot of social dance and step, but for me, "Kaleidoscope" needed to be more abstract, so there was a modern-dance language I brought in. When it came to "Girl on Fire," I didn't want to do the same thing. At first, the movement I was generating was too reminiscent of "Kaleidoscope," and it wasn't pushing the story forward. I was thinking of the dancers as people in the space. Then I thought, *What if the fire represents an element—which it is—and what if the dancers are representations of that fire?* That was the aha moment for me, because once I allowed myself to think further than them being actual people in the space, I was able to crack that.

Heidi Griffiths, casting director
Dance is a character in *Hell's Kitchen*. It's often said that when humans want to express their emotion, they speak. And when speaking is no longer enough, they sing. And when singing can no longer hold the emotion, they dance. When Reid Clarke and David Guzman come out and do the "Work On It" duet, it's so joyous. It feels like everything that I remember New York in the '90s being: the freedom and the color and the sound and all of it. It's cheeky and glorious, and I adore that moment.

Most of the show's costumes are realistic representations of what people wore in the '90s, but for the dancers in "Kaleidoscope," Dede Ayite executed silhouettes of the era in iridescent fabrics. "That moment was like a waking dream for Ali, seeing things come to life that she's never seen before," says Alicia Keys. "Dede illuminated that through the colors and brightness."

ON ROOM

MAKEUP INSPO

MICHAEL CLIFTON, MAKEUP DESIGNER

For inspiration, I pulled from pop culture references like hip-hop, R&B, and rap artists of the time, as well as popular actors and actresses. But also, textures and colors that you see in the street.

In terms of looks, for the teenagers it was definitely Lip Liner Palooza. Very dark, very defined. It was a statement. To make it more '90s, we thinned out the eyebrows. Now we have very full brows, but back then it was very thin. These kids didn't have a lot of money for makeup. Most of them probably wouldn't wear a lot of it anyway, but if they did, eyebrow pencil was also going to be their lip liner because we don't have a lot of money here. So I was creating a look that looked like products were multitaskers in that way.

Jersey and her friends, the grown-up people, still had touches of the '80s, So the colors on those ladies were a bit brighter: They could have more fun, and they would match their nails to their lipstick.

This is not a makeup show, per se. Alicia didn't want to do this costumey, fakey version of the neighborhood, so everything needed to be authentic. I would come to the table with all my ideas and then scale back 50% because it needed to be real and gritty, but also turned up enough that it read for stage. My job was finding that fine balance, and it was trial and error a lot of times. For example, with Maleah, who plays Ali, we're both fans of a glowy, pretty cheek. We were seeing how far we could go with the blush before Michael Greif said anything. For our first dress rehearsal, the dressing room didn't have the best lighting, so we went a little too far with the blush. In those early photos, her cheeks are screaming. We were like, *Let's take that back a little bit.*

Michael Clifton's face charts for [clockwise from top left] Jackie Leon, Reid Clarke, Maleah Joi Moon, and Chloe Davis

JACKIE

REID

CHLOE

MALEAH

5

STAGING NEW YORK LIVES

This page: The dance ensemble during "Empire State of Mind"
Previous page: Maleah Joi Moon and ensemble performing "The Gospel"

Along with costumes and choreography, the authenticity of Ali's world had to be conveyed through set, projection, and lighting design. Audiences needed to feel the soaring height of the Plaza tower, the cramped quarters of the apartment, the excitement and edginess of the streets. Audiences needed to see New York.

Chris Lee (Knuck) jokes that the city is the show's best supporting actor. "New York is arguably number two on the call sheet," he says. For a set that accurately conveyed the spirit of 1990s Hell's Kitchen, there had to be grit, there had to be a sense of community, and there had to be a transportive quality—the audience had to feel they could move from the forty-second floor to the sidewalk in the blink of a spotlight. Michael Greif called in designers who could give the city the star status it deserved: projection designer Peter Nigrini, lighting designer Natasha Katz, and scenic designer Robert Brill.

PROJECTION AND LIGHTING DESIGN

To deliver the rich textures of Ali's world, especially in scenes that took place outdoors, Michael knew he wanted to work with Peter Nigrini, a leader in the still-emerging field of projection design.

Michael Greif, director
I had worked with Peter on a number of things, but most recently *Dear Evan Hansen*. I think he is an artist of the greatest magnitude who has an extraordinary response to music and rhythm but also a keen understanding of dramaturgy. He's really great.

Kris Diaz, book writer
Peter is genius. He is one of those Broadway legends that walk among us.

Peter Nigrini, projection designer
People talk about how TV and movies have made us less smart. That may be true in a sense, but they have also made every audience so much more sophisticated when it comes to understanding visual storytelling and visual language. My function in this production is to allow the storytelling to move at a cinematic pace, not a traditional theatrical pace. That requires this ever-shifting visual landscape. We're not making a movie, it is still a live experience, but we're providing all those visual cues that you might see in a film to create informational responses like, *Where are we? When? How do we slither from Gramercy Park back to Manhattan Plaza in ten seconds?* In a traditional theatrical language, people would spend a lot of time talking about that or physically changing sets.

Using video clips and still shots as virtual components of the set, Peter and his studio of animators created projections that ranged from sweeping skylines to graffiti walls, vegetable stands to hippie-filled parks. Oversized lettering and abstract graphics added additional layers of information and mood.

Peter Nigrini
Projection language can provide an incredible richness—and not just in the plumbing of, *Where are we? When are we?* Locations are an emotional part of the story.

Alicia Keys
Michael was very much pushing the projections, but I was worried that they were going to feel false in this space. In music land, when I go on tour, projections are meant to be flashy. They're meant to be seen from 15,000 seats above. You do it so that you can keep up the energy. But Peter showed me how it could be quite subtle, grounding you in what each neighborhood looks and feels like.

Peter Nigrini
There was a lot of nervousness about our design before our first day onstage at the Public. We'd had some difficulty in getting everyone to understand where we were headed—partly because the set is

Mockups for the projection design

Maleah Joi Moon (Ali) and the ensemble in front of the Manhattan Plaza projection

all black. There is not a thing on that stage that isn't black, except the couch. Understandably, it was hard for Alicia and Kris and Oskar to see past all this black scenery to what we were imagining, which is full of color and light.

Michael told me that Oskar Eustis pulled him aside at one point and said, "I'm very worried. Where's the color? Where's the richness? Where's the vibrancy of New York and the neighborhood?" And Michael's response was, "Don't worry, we have Peter," which was such a great compliment. He told me this before I knew we had succeeded—so it was both a compliment and a little bit of, "You better deliver."

The day the cast first walked onto the stage and Alicia came into the theater, we had projections set up with images of Manhattan Plaza and the courtyard. It was such a joy to see everyone discover the neighborhood that we'd built for them, saying, "Oh yeah, look at the bodega!" We'd been sharing those details in storyboard form, but until it was at full scale, it was hard to grasp. That was a great reveal. When Ali is coming down in the elevator, there's not much there. It's really spare. That's intentional. She walks out the doors of Manhattan Plaza, and all of a sudden, the whole neighborhood comes to life.

Mandy Hackett, co-producer

When I first saw "Gramercy Park," with all its saturated yellows and blues, it was so striking. When I started at the Public there was no projection design. It didn't exist. Peter has been at the forefront of the field from the beginning, and he's really been able to grow that art form.

Michael Greif

One example of Peter's work, in collaboration with lighting designer Natasha Katz, is the color palette of "Gospel." The stage explodes in quick graphic color blocks, which matches the energy of the choreography. There's a wonderful synergy between what the choreography is doing, what the music is doing, and what Peter is doing visually.

There are ways in which Peter helps significantly with storytelling. There's a shift in "No One" where the chorus shows up in Jersey and Ali's apartment. I love that they show up and how that breaks open the song, but it's a very realistic scene. So Peter designed a visual representation of people peering into windows in order to explain to the audience why the chorus is in the apartment. *Oh, I get it. They're the neighbors.*

The visual subtlety in many of the scenes is underscored by the carefully calibrated palette, positioning, and timing of the theater's lighting.

Natasha Katz, lighting designer

There's so much that has to do with emotion in lighting. Lighting designers are like film editors in the sense

PROJECTIONS
THE ELLINGTON ROOM

To capture the spiritual and thematic importance of the Ellington Room—a multipurpose space in Manhattan Plaza where Alicia Keys learned piano and took part in recitals—the show's creative team had to think outside the box. "Our goal was to jump away from the realistic in that room, which was less than impressive in real life," says projection designer Peter Nigrini, "and create what ultimately could feel almost like a chapel or a sacred space that is about history, ancestors, art, and music."

The real Ellington Room was a utilitarian, orange-walled, venetian-blinded, architecturally unremarkable space; Robert Brill's minimalist stage version contains only a piano and bench. For the more heightened emotional moments, lighting designer Natasha Katz dramatically spotlights Ali and Miss Liza Jane, thrusting the rest of the stage into shadow. In two instances, dialogue between the two characters is augmented by documentary footage that spans the back of the stage.

The first real-life moment occurs at the end of Act One while Miss Liza Jane sings the devastating

Vivian Strong

"Perfect Way to Die." As Ali watches her mentor give voice to rage, a montage of images depicting actual victims of police brutality flashes by in fragments. Peter, along with six animators from his design studio, designed the projections after securing permission from survivors of the victims to feature their images. "Alicia wanted to convey that this was not fiction," Nigrini says. "It's a very specific political commentary."

The other use of documentary imagery comes in the second act as Miss Liza Jane rushes to impart as much as she can in the limited time she has left. "You are but the latest branch on a long-standing tree," she says to Ali. Archival images of historic Black women pianists Florence Price, Margaret Bonds, and Hazel Scott appear with the scratches and dings of old newsreels as Miss Liza Jane demonstrates each woman's distinct playing style.

Peter, Alicia, and Michael Greif deliberated at length whether bringing in documentary information would pull audiences out of the experience, but they eventually concluded that it pushed the story forward in a useful way. "It was more important to the bigger emotional arc of the show to include those images," Peter says. "They showed something else going on besides the struggle of a seventeen-year-old girl, which is an important and valuable struggle, but there's a bigger story as well. It's us, the authors, speaking to the audience, but it's also the machine of the show speaking to Ali about coming of age and who she is, and the magnitude—or lack of—of her personal problems. We would never have done that anywhere but the Ellington Room. The nature of that room made that possible.

Mockups for the projections during "Perfect Way to Die"

Phillip Pannell

The cast during "Hallelujah/Like Water"

that we can tell the audience where to look. I can light downstage right, and you won't see any other part of the stage. We can light somebody's face, or we can put them into silhouette. In *Hell's Kitchen*, a lot of the light comes from a very low angle in order to sculpt the body, so that you see all the muscles and the beautiful bodies of the dancers.

Natasha's work not only attends to the audience's visual experience, but also the storytelling that comes across through music. Shifts in projection and lighting regularly key to the tempo and progression of each song.

Natasha Katz
I might grab a drumbeat and have the lights pulsate underneath it. The audience wouldn't know it, but it all adds emotionally and subliminally to what they are feeling. There are so many songs and so many dances that are propulsive, and they're lit brightly and in different colors. As the music changes, the color changes. If there's a key change, it goes into a completely different look.

In Act Two, after we've been seeing these dancers' bodies in full, colorful light, we get to the funeral. I'm still using the same low angle of light coming from the side, but now it is touching their bodies with a little kiss of light, so that you just see the people's outlines, so that you feel the grief. Camille has some incredible dance going on at the time, but it's illuminated with just a pencil-thin bit of light on the dancers so that you feel it, but it's not overwhelming the story.

SET DESIGN

For the physical set design, Michael turned to Robert Brill. The two had collaborated previously on *Monster*, a play by Neal Bell, and Robert worked with Peter Nigrini on the Temptations musical, *Ain't Too Proud*.

Alicia Keys
Michael was excited to work with Robert Brill from the beginning. They've worked together before, they know each other's vibe, and Robert has personal connections to the building, so there was all that synergy surrounding the set design. It was clear that Robert had a high level of awareness about Manhattan Plaza and the neighborhood.

Not only had Robert and his family lived in Hell's Kitchen for several years, but his daughter also attended preschool in the basement of a Plaza tower and had friends who lived in the apartments above. Brill had been an eyewitness to Ali's world and the sharp contrasts of its physical spaces.

Alicia Keys
We talked a lot about creating the oppression Ali feels through structure. If you look at the Manhattan Plaza

buildings, they're very big, they're very ominous. They take up a lot of space, and we really wanted to play on that.

Robert Brill, scenic designer
One of the biggest challenges was capturing the complexity of New York City. Michael, in his direction, was also clear that he didn't want it to look like a postcard. And while we do deliver some of those "postcard" moments at the end—especially with "Empire State of Mind"—they're always presented in a fractured way. There's a constant play of different scales, proportions, colors, and densities, viewed through a layered collage of complex shapes.

The idea for the set began with a conversation I had with Michael about Manhattan Plaza, which is a character in the story itself. We knew we needed a sense of fluidity to move easily from one location to another and didn't want to be encumbered by "realistic" scenery. We focused on the essential elements, gestures and visual cues that would give the feeling of Manhattan Plaza without relying on strict realism.

Robert introduced two skeletal towers that flank the stage and a series of spare balconies, all of which are automated and move side to side as well as upstage and downstage. Lines painted on the floor of the stage suggest avenues and streets, and the collective dynamic of actors and objects and projected images crossing paths evokes the bustle of the city.

Robert Brill
New York is a constantly shifting landscape, where buildings and spaces evolve as you move through them. So much is out of your control, shaped by the energy and movement of the people around you. It's a living collage that's both disorienting and wonderfully overwhelming.

A close-up of the set

Michael Greif
Robert Brill is a wonderful artist, and he landed on the notion of depicting Manhattan Plaza through a series of terraces. The set design is pretty simple, which is something I gravitate toward. But I also knew that the projections would be carrying a lot of the day, and I would be dependent on Robert for figuring out the stuff that the actors physically deal with.

Robert Brill
The band was an important part of our early conversations. Could we feature the musicians onstage to reflect the community Ali grew up in—a vibrant, layered hive of culture? It felt important to surround Ali with the real, living presence of the artists who shaped her childhood.

Michael Greif
One question was, where do we put the vocal ensemble when they are part of solos and duets in which they're not playing a realistic part? We had this notion of elevating them, similar to what you've seen in *RENT* and other shows. They almost feel like thought bubbles when they're elevated—like an extension of the person's thoughts. So our ask was, how do we create a series of levels people can stand on, and Robert came up with these bridges that move.

And there's the multilevel scaffolding that Knuck works on, which was a wonderful way to enliven those Knuck-Ali ballads visually. I loved the idea of them going somewhere, and I imagined, especially for "Unthinkable," that this scaffold became their little island within the island.

Chris Lee, actor (Knuck)
The set is minimalistic, so it's the energy you have to believe. When Knuck's on a scaffold, it's about the way he's talking to Ali. Michael let me block a lot of my own scenes and pick all the props we use. One day, I was just like, okay, I need paintbrushes. I want tarps. I want to climb up and down. I want to jump off. I want to be busy, because he's got this job to do.

Aziza Miller, keyboard 2
I am afraid of heights. The first time I saw those towers, and saw that piano up there, I said, "Oh, my God, I'm going to fall through the opening. I'm going to pass out. I can't do this." But I never expressed that because I'm a fighter. I thought, *Well, I'm not going to be the one crying, not out loud. I may go home and cry, but I'm going to master this.* I looked at it as leveling up, learning. This was a whole new experience. It was a

BROADWAY'S BEST

On April 20, 2024, *Hell's Kitchen* opened at the legendary Sam S. Shubert Theatre. This theater has been home to many successful and long-running productions, including *A Chorus Line* (which also had its start at the Public Theater and then played at the Shubert for a record-setting fifteen years, from 1975 to 1990).

You couldn't do better than this venue in terms of delivering the full Broadway experience. Even the five-story building is dramatic: The Shubert reigns over the corner of Forty-Fourth Street and Shubert Alley, allowing for marquees that are visible from two directions. Its Venetian Renaissance exterior is clad in brick and terra-cotta with plaster frescoes. Inside, the lobby has vaulted ceilings and a marble mosaic tile floor, and the auditorium—with triple the seating capacity of the Public's largest theater—features elaborate plasterwork and classically themed murals that surround a proscenium stage. Most of Broadway's forty-one theaters have only two seating levels, but the Shubert has three. Both its mezzanine and balcony are cantilevered, so no sightline is interrupted by support columns. Every seat is a good seat.

Alicia Keys never questioned the value of starting out at the Public, but Broadway was part of her dream from the start. Toward that end, even before Public rehearsals were underway, executive producer Aaron Lustbader and the Public's associate artistic director (and later *Hell's Kitchen* co-producer) Mandy Hackett began exploring options. "Our job was to speak to the Broadway theater owners and see what was available," Aaron says, "because if there's no real estate, it doesn't matter how great the show is."

Aaron and Mandy identified several theaters whose schedule aligned with theirs, but the Shubert looked to be the best fit. Its three seating areas give the feel of being part of a smaller audience, which allows playgoers to maintain a more intimate connection to Ali as she takes them through her journey.

"I've always loved the Shubert," Mandy says, "and it has always been my dream to do a show there." Of the seventeen shows she had transferred from the Public to Broadway before *Hell's Kitchen*, none had landed here. Until now.

Alicia in front of the Shubert Theatre

challenge. Now, when I'm not playing, I'm twirling on my chair and looking at the actors. I'm good.

At the top of the first act, when Ali stands inside a simple rectangular frame, audiences instantly understand that she's riding her building's elevator, descending from the forty-second floor. The sense of her vertical journey comes across through enormous floor numbers projected on an upstage screen as well as through graphic lines of light that simulate Ali's movement through space. It's immersive but not obtrusive, which was everyone's goal.

Robert Brill
As we began our collaboration, the opportunity to capture the scope and scale of New York also posed many questions. Was it too big? Was that even possible? Would the thrilling proportions of a city get in the way of a very intimate story? After seeing the show many times, those concerns have faded. The design feels like a true reflection of New York—full of complexity, movement, and just the right amount of danger. Not only in the shifting pieces on stage, but in the intricate structure that holds it all together.

I was initially nervous about doing a play set in New York while being in New York itself. The city is right outside, so there's no separation, and it invites comparison—people might think, "That's not what New York feels like." But I've never felt that way. Instead, the experience has felt just as intense and demanding as navigating the city itself, and that's been incredibly satisfying.

Maleah Joi Moon rehearsing with a set piece representing the Manhattan Plaza elevator

Maleah Joi Moon and Chris Lee rehearsing "Gramercy Park" with a scaffold

Alicia Keys
Robert's structures dynamically created dimensions and spaces, and even though you feel the movement, you're not really paying attention to it. It's not like shows I've seen where too much is happening and it feels chaotic. In this space, the set change is happening, but it's transforming in this slick way while you're transfixed on what's happening with the actors and dancers.

Robert Brill
When all the elements of design align—Natasha's lighting, Peter's video artistry, Dede's costumes, and Gareth's sound—it doesn't feel like separate pieces. It feels like everything is working together, fully in sync, as one cohesive whole.

HK

WHO WAS YOUR MENTOR?

SHOSHANA BEAN ON BARBARA IRVIN

Mine was 100% without question my voice teacher, Barbara Irvin. She came into my life when I was about ten years old. I did a professional production in Portland, Oregon, of *Sunday in the Park with George*, and she played the nurse. She was also a voice teacher, and my mom approached her and said, "Will you train my daughter?" Barbara said, "I don't train little girls until they're of a certain age." They had to pass puberty or whatever. I think my mom pushed a little bit and was like, "Please. I don't know what to do with her. All she wants to do is sing. And I know she's good." Barbara said, "You know what? I'll make an exception, because you're right. She is special. I'll do it. If it doesn't work, I'm going to tell you, but I will at least give it a shot." I was with Barbara from the time I was eleven or twelve through when I went to college. Even when I would come home to visit, I would get a lesson in, just to be with my hometown teacher. I don't know what I would be without her. She really showed me what my voice was capable of. I had no idea. I thought, *This is what I do and how I do it*. But she said, "No, my dear, there's this whole other spectrum of colors. You haven't even scratched the surface." She trained me classically. She exposed me to Sondheim's catalog. She told me that I could go to school for musical theater, and which schools were the ones to go to. She put my train on the tracks. She's my Miss Liza Jane.

AARON LUSTBADER ON CARL PASBJERG

In my first general-management job, I was assigned to work for a man named Carl Pasbjerg. He was really interested in mentoring someone, which is very rare in our space, and so he let me follow him everywhere, become a mini version of himself. There was rarely a moment where he would say, "I need to do this privately." I had been an English major at Cornell, and so I would write what, by his standards, were flowery sentences or paragraphs. He would take a red pen—literally a red pen—and edit my business memos to be more formal until I picked up on it myself. Now, I will say I have since come back to my English major-ness in my business communications, because people actually enjoy the context and the humanity of that. But regardless, he spent a lot of time on it and on me.

PETER NIGRINI ON PAMELA HOWARD

One of the strongest influences I've had in my theatrical career is a woman named Pamela Howard. She's a British scenographer, and for a number of years she ran a course at the Central Saint Martins College of Art and Design in London, where I studied and received a master's degree. I began that process proposing a thesis that would explore how projection could be a live and interactive medium in theater. I arrived at this course to discover that Pamela hated the idea of projection in the theater. She clearly didn't hate it enough to not accept me into the program, but in no uncertain terms, she felt that it was untheatrical.

She was so unbelievably committed to the craft of theater and to her students that upon my graduation, she had one recommendation for me: "I know you're very interested in photography, perhaps you should pursue that."

What was so helpful about that was that she genuinely believed I was not on a path to success, and she was giving me her honest, unvarnished advice. That is what a mentor needs to do. She didn't believe in what I was doing, so the last thing I needed was her telling me that I should do it. The other great thing is, she taught me that at the end of the day, I needed to do what I needed to do. If she had been able to change my mind, then she would have been right.

CAMILLE A. BROWN ON ROGER C. JEFFREY

One of my mentors is Roger C. Jeffrey, a dance teacher and choreographer who danced with Twyla Tharp. Roger and I went to the same dance school in Queens. He's only about five years older than me, but he was my teacher at one point, so he was someone we all looked up to. He became a friend and a brother and a mentor, and we've stayed connected.

When I auditioned for Juilliard, I was wait-listed, and I called him. I was really upset. He said, "The school doesn't make you. You make you." And I never forgot that. I tell him all the time, "You need to write a book," because he just gives jewels. When you're sitting there watching him teach class, at a certain point you're like, "I need a notepad to take down these things he's saying, because these are not just dance school lessons. These are life lessons."

ROBERT BRILL ON DES MCANUFF

The renowned director Des McAnuff has played a pivotal role in shaping my career. Beyond being colleagues, we've become good friends over nearly thirty-five years of collaboration, having worked together on more than twenty productions. It often feels like I'm constantly involved in a project with Des, and every time I do, it's like attending a master class.

I often share with my students the saying: "If you're the smartest person in the room, you're in the wrong room." When I'm working with Des, I always know I'm exactly where I belong—surrounded by wonderful collaborators, pushing boundaries and making work at the top of their game.

KECIA LEWIS ON RUTHEL KOEHLER

I said yes to this role in part because I have had so many Miss Liza Janes in my life that I am so very grateful for. One was Ruthel Koehler. She was my voice and diction and acting teacher in my sophomore year at the original High School of Performing Arts, which later became LaGuardia.

What Mrs. Koehler gave me was a very sober understanding of what the craft of acting could bring to the world. She spoke in broad terms about the importance of representing. When you play a character, you're representing many people who are that person in the world. You want to think of the character in that way, so they need to be fleshed out enough, and you have to do the work so that every aspect of who this person is, as much as you can pull out of yourself or observe and utilize, can be put into this character, so that when people see this character, they represent somebody we all know.

I am actually doing an imitation of Mrs. Koehler in my speech pattern as Miss Liza Jane. I'm still close with a lot of the people I went to high school with, and some have come to see the show. Afterwards, all of them have asked me, "Are you doing Mrs. Koehler? I hear Mrs. Koehler." Yes, I am absolutely doing her.

6

THE DREAM LIFTS OFF

This page: Alicia Keys on opening night

Previous page: Kecia Lewis as Miss Liza Jane with Maleah Joi Moon as Ali

THE CURTAINS GO UP

On October 24, 2023, *Hell's Kitchen* opened in the 300-seat Newman Theater, the largest of the Public's six stages. Most shows that have transferred from the Public to Broadway got their start at the Newman, including *A Chorus Line*, *Hamilton*, *Fun Home*, and *Girl from the North Country*.

After the premiere, critics praised the show for its reimagined songs, stunning vocals, spectacular choreography, and powerful visual landscape of costumes, sets, projections, and lighting. They noted the wit of Kris Diaz's book and the steady hand of director Michael Greif. Reviewers described the musical as "soaring" and "irresistible," and the trade publication *Variety* wrote: "*Hell's Kitchen* is a sparkling story paying homage to New York, to the beautiful and heartbreaking transition between girlhood and womanhood and to the women who hold our hands through it all." Even those who had criticisms—particularly of the second act—saw it as promising and deservedly Broadway-bound. Audiences loved it.

Oskar Eustis, artistic director, Public Theater
They adored it, leapt to their feet. One of the difficulties we faced, and it was a good one to have, was that the audience loved it so much we couldn't keep a ticket in the house. We could've run it for two years, which wouldn't have made any sense, since we lost money every week. Financially it would have been a disaster.

The Public did extend the original run by five weeks, but even a sold-out 300-seat theater couldn't bring in enough income to offset ongoing production costs.

Oskar Eustis
Here's where I'm incredibly proud of the discipline and brains of this team, led by Michael Greif. Even though every ticket sold immediately, Michael never had any illusion that the show had reached its final form.

Michael Greif, director
Broadway is always the dream; it's always the hope. But the only flop I've ever had—and maybe I'm being arrogant by saying there was only one—was a show that didn't have an earlier incarnation at a regional theater or at a nonprofit in New York. Other directors can succeed without that, but I found that the only way I can succeed is if there's a production prior to Broadway.

Aaron Lustbader, executive producer
When I came on board, which was shortly before the Public rehearsals started, I said to everyone, "It's taken twelve years to get to this moment. There will be a lot of people who just want to get it on Broadway, but make sure the show's ready. Be careful and protect it, because if it needs more development work, you have to build the ability to do that into the schedule."

At the end of our very first preview, I was crying, and other people were crying, and we were so excited. There was so much energy in the choreography. There were such surprises in how the music was utilized and placed. It was such a love letter to New York. It had all the beats.

Shortly after that, though, we all came to understand that the show wasn't yet completely jelling. To get it to a place where it was likely to be a hit, the creative team would have to make a thousand nips and tucks.

The schedule for making adjustments turned out to be a tight one. Even before the show opened at the Public, Aaron Lustbader and Mandy Hackett, who had shifted into the role of co-producer, managed to secure not just any Broadway theater, but the 1,457-seat Sam S. Shubert Theatre, which many consider the theater district's crown jewel. The new venue had greater ceiling height and automation capabilities than the Newman, which allowed Robert Brill to fully execute his vision for the set.

Robert Brill, scenic designer
New York often feels like being in a canyon—a concrete canyon. At the Public Theater, we had to work within tight height restrictions, which meant finding creative ways to suggest the scale of New York in a smaller

setting. Our move to the Shubert Theatre gave us an exciting opportunity to truly capture the majesty and height of the city.

Mandy Hackett, co-producer
Beyond the height, the size of the entire theater made a big difference. The show needed to breathe a little more. It needed the whole theater—audience included.

Aaron Lustbader
Another set change we made was to add LED tape onto the edges of all the towers, which allowed Peter Nigrini to add a huge spectrum of color and vividness.

Michael, Alicia, and Kris brainstormed about what needed work, particularly in terms of fleshing out characters.

Michael Greif
We wanted to enrich Ali's bond with Knuck and get them playing together, so that the relationship and her music were a little more fused. The way in which they now hang out together in the Ellington Room is new in the Broadway version, as is the little kernel of mentorship that's suggested when they talk about drummers.

Kate Murray, casting director
Knuck talking to Ali about drummers was a lovely deepening of the script. It put him up there with the artists in her life, like her father, like Miss Liza Jane.

Chris Lee, actor (Knuck)
We cut songs, and that hurt because we were attached, but it was better. We cleaned things. We made things make more sense. We got to the point. It was two handfuls of small changes that made a big difference.

Kecia Lewis, actor (Miss Liza Jane)
Miss Liza Jane was brought a bit more into Ali's life. Now there's a scene with Ali after I speak to Jersey, and we also have that little piano lesson in the middle of "Girl on Fire." Neither was there Off-Broadway.

Shoshana Bean, actor (Jersey)
When I knew we were moving to Broadway, I called Michael and said, "We've got to talk. There are things in this script that are not working for me. My goal is to make Jersey as rich and full and as nuanced as she can be, and here are my thoughts." He was wildly open to that, which was great.

Michael Greif
It was a great conversation, and it was direct and honest. Shoshana pointed out three or four events, and they were all solvable. In some cases, I needed to share the process with Kris and Alicia, but there was tremendous excitement about these refinements all around.

One of Shoshana's concerns was that the proximity of the dance ensemble for "Pawn It All" would

Chris Lee as Knuck with Maleah Joi Moon as Ali during "Girl on Fire"

Shoshana Bean and Maleah Joi Moon during the curtain call on opening night

exaggerate what was meant to be an intimate dramatic moment. To more firmly anchor the scene in reality, the dancers moved from the stage floor to the towers, which also cleared the path for Jersey's approach to Davis and the men in the jazz club.

Michael Greif
Then there were also some refinements to the scene with Liza Jane, which is one of my favorites in the whole play. Shoshana always accepted the fact that Jersey's rudeness toward Miss Liza was coming out of an extreme emotional desperation, but the level of rudeness troubled her. I said, "Just make sure that what you're doing is going for help. And because you're so bad at asking for help, it comes out all wrong. But you're not condemning this woman. You're begging her to help." Then I went and talked to Kris about it, and he made small textual tweaks. We took those back to Shoshana, and there was happiness.

Sometimes, you'll hear from an actor, "I want to do this," and you're like, "Oh, Jesus Christ, how are we going to make that work?" Or "How am I going to be able to say no to that?" Everything Shoshana mentioned immediately registered as wonderful things to pursue. It was so keen and acute and right.

Even with Brandon Victor Dixon's exquisitely nuanced performance, the Davis character was tricky to calibrate. For Broadway, Davis's relationship to Ali evolved slightly, and Jersey's attitude toward him was more firmly anchored in her daughter's need to connect *with* him than her own need to protect Ali *from* him.

Michael Greif
We had talked a lot about how, after "Pawn It All," Jersey invites Davis to dinner. At the Public, we looked at the beautiful song he sings at Liza Jane's funeral and the comments he makes about being a better person and thought those were enough to justify the invitation. Many other people didn't.

Kris fashioned a little more for Davis to say to Ali after the funeral, and when Jersey sees her daughter need her father, that does it. "Pawn It All" is a big deal, but every parent knows your kid can make you reverse anything in a second.

The team also had to figure out a clear justification for Davis to show up for the "Empire" finale, which brings everyone onstage and segues into the curtain call.

Michael Greif
It's theatrical necessity for Davis to be there. The whole company needs to show up. Even dead Liza Jane shows up. So we continued to look for ways in which he could be given permission to return.

WHO IS YOUR JERSEY?

At the end of *Hell's Kitchen*, Ali finally recognizes how steadfastly her mother, Jersey, has loved and protected her over the years. Just before they sing "No One," Ali says to Jersey, "Ma, you're here. You've always been here. Thank you."

In many ways, *Hell's Kitchen* differs from Alicia Keys's own story. But Ali having Jersey in her corner is absolutely drawn from real life: Alicia's mom, Terria Joseph, was, is, and always will be a fierce champion of her daughter's dreams. "I didn't always know how to be a parent," Terria says, "but because I was an artist and she seemed to be gravitating toward that, I said, 'Let me just try and help her.'"

The *Hell's Kitchen* world is full of talented artists who were fortunate enough to have that unwavering support. Here, three of them—Vanessa Ferguson (Tiny), Kris Diaz (book writer), and Maleah Joi Moon (Ali)—speak to the people who were there when their dreams began.

VANESSA FERGUSON

Vanessa jokes that she was raised in the "family orphanage," a two-bedroom apartment on Brooklyn's Kings Highway. Her grandmother, Doris McRae, took in offspring on an as-needed basis: During Vanessa's New York years, five grandchildren were under the one roof. "I wasn't going to let anybody be hungry if they needed me," says the matriarch known as Mommy Doris, who early on recognized Vanessa's musical talents.

Mommy Doris was born with a great voice of her own. At 13, she ran away from her home in North Carolina to go to New York City. She dreamed of singing with Duke Ellington's band at the Apollo Theater, but life took her in another direction. Now 95 and living in Greensboro, North Carolina, Mommy Doris still sings at the drop of a hat. "Most people never forget me," she says.

Vanessa Do you remember when my musical abilities first showed themselves?

Doris McRae We were always singing in the house, so I wasn't paying that much attention. But when you sang in that school talent show, I was completely carried away. I said to myself, I *didn't know that girl could sing like that.* You remember the year, Vanessa?

Vanessa Probably 1996. I was ten or eleven.

Doris I didn't know what you were going to do.

Vanessa Nobody knew. I kept it a secret. I had realized

Vanessa Ferguson with her grandmother, Doris McRae

that I could sing, and I wanted everyone to be shocked when they heard me. My friend Deidra sang the first part of "Killing Me Softly" on a little stage in the lunchroom. I had a cordless microphone, and I came from the back of the room singing the second verse. That's how you heard me before you saw me. It was the Fugees version, and it was the hottest song out at the time. By the end, all the kids were standing up on the tables.

Doris I hear the voice, I look around, and here comes Vanessa. And I'm telling you, I couldn't believe it.

Vanessa But did it shock you, really? You're an amazing singer, and my mother was an amazing singer.

Doris Yes, it was truly unbelievable. "Killing Me Softly" is still my favorite song.

Vanessa Mommy, you never told me this, and I've known you forty years now. How did you afford that Roland keyboard you bought for me when I was eight years old? It was a $2,000 keyboard.

Doris We put it on layaway because we couldn't just go in the store and buy it outright. We weren't able to do that. But I was determined that you were going to have it, because every time you went to church, you couldn't keep your hands off the piano.

Vanessa And how did you manage to pay for my weekly piano lessons?

Doris I collected from everyone in the family for you kids. Everyone contributed to the household, and this way I could save a little.

Vanessa So you paid for the piano lessons by ...?

Doris It wasn't easy. It was sacrificing one thing to do another. But Vanessa, I would have, I don't want to say rob a bank, but you loved that piano. You wanted it so bad, and I wanted you to have it.

Vanessa A lot of times a music career would be frowned upon. There's no guarantee you're going to make it. You didn't have those concerns?

Doris I never thought about that, because you were truly amazing. You just kept on surprising me and shocking me with things I didn't know you could do. And you've always been on the stage. What was that other play you were in when you were wearing a hat?

Vanessa You put me in community theater when I was fourteen, and I was Clarissa Crow in *Aesop's Falables*. That was the one musical I had done before *Hell's Kitchen*. Outside of that, I did talent shows, sang in church, did weddings, sang wherever I could. There literally is no me without you, Mommy Doris, and not just genetically. You gave me this ability and the love for music. You put me in piano lessons.

Doris I put you and your sister into music lessons because I didn't have the chance to have the career I wanted. I didn't have any support.

KRIS DIAZ

Kris was raised twenty miles north of New York City, but his parents, Linda and Ken Diaz, had grown up there and they visited often. During Kris's childhood, Linda worked in purchasing and Ken climbed poles for the phone company. They didn't make their living in the performing arts, but Linda had been fascinated by musical theater since childhood, and Ken was game to support his son's passions.

Kris Diaz Ma, you're how I got into theater. Everything starts from your interest. Do you want to talk about that? You weren't pushing me into it, like, "Oh, you're gonna make theater someday." It was just present.

Linda Diaz As a kid, I used to visit the local library in the South Bronx. For some reason I was attracted to the play section. I read every book of every musical from the '40s, '50s, and '60s. I could sing every song, I could read every line. Obviously, at that time, I never went to the theater other than plays they did in school. But once you were about seven years old, I decided I was going to take you to plays, and we started going to children's theater.

Kris You took me to see theater, and Dad took me to stuff I wanted to do, like baseball and wrestling.

Linda I was really surprised when you got to high school and joined the drama club.

Ken Diaz Then you and your friends started your own theater company outside of school. That was a big effort, and it went on for two years.

Kris We called it Great Beyond Broadway Productions. We got access to an abandoned auditorium, and somebody said, "If you clean it out, you can put up shows in here."

Linda It was like a Mickey Rooney movie. "Let's put on a show."

Kris Dad, you would make all the programs, and you two were the company parents.

Linda I think there were dollars involved.

Kris I'm sure there were dollars. It was very low-budget, no frills, but there were definitely dollars involved.

Linda It was fun for me. Several moms cleaned out closets for costumes. We fed everyone at rehearsals. Mainly, you kids did it on your own. That was the big deal to us. You were dedicated. Still, I never expected it to turn into a career for you.

Kris Once it became clear that I was interested in musicals, do you remember how that changed how we spent time together, Mom? Starting when I was fifteen?

Linda We did a lot of Broadway shows. We got hooked on a couple. *Crazy for You* was over and over. *Chicago* was over and over. We went to see something on a Wednesday matinee, and we were left a little wanting, so I said to you, "Do you want to do a *Crazy for You*?" Your dad came and met us, and we did a twofer that day.

Kris That day they were like, *We're into it. We're gonna go again.* And my dad is not a theater dude. And that's the day I made the conscious decision: This is what I'm doing. I thought, *I really love this thing. I really care about it. And my parents are in.*

Linda I don't remember knowing you were serious until you started at NYU. I asked, "What's your major going to be?" You said, "Theater." And I was like, *Yeah, I did it. I got him mixed up in theater.*

Ken One of our friends said, "Does it bother you that

A young Kris Diaz (right) with his mother, Linda, and his father, Ken

Kris didn't major in business at college?" My response was that I would support him until the age of forty, as long as he was passionate about what he did.

Kris Dad, it's not just that you were supportive of me. When we first started looking at schools, I thought I'd study finance. You said, "Why do you want to go to business school?" I said, "I'm supposed to make money." And you talked me out of it. You said, "Go to school for something that you care about." Basically, *Get smart*.

Ken If you get off the track for whatever reason, you end up doing something you don't want to do.

Kris When you have that level of support, when so much time, effort, money, and care have been put into it, it's like, "How am I *not* gonna do this?"

Linda I'm not going to say I was worried, but I did think, *It's a tough business*, and *how's he going to survive financially?* I was concerned about the criticism and whether you'd get support from the theater community. So yes, I did think of those things. On the other hand, I always said, "Damn, he's good."

MALEAH JOI MOON

Steve Moon put headphones on his wife's pregnant belly and serenaded baby Maleah with music. He

played her Mozart and Sam Cook, Tina Marie and Tina Turner, Aretha Franklin and, yes, Alicia Keys.

Steve Moon You've always had a beautiful voice. The voice was a nice pitch. You had these fluctuations in it that are so beautiful to me. But what blew me away was the first time I saw you act.

Maleah I was in sixth grade, and my friends were all doing *The Wizard of Oz* at school. Auditions came up, and I was like, *I want to hang out with my friends. I'll be a tree. That's fine.* Then I got the role of Dorothy, and me being the little perfectionist kid that I was, I was gonna take my straight A-ness into the theater part of my life. I studied my lines all the time and was super excited to go to rehearsal.

Steve You landed in very good hands. Your teacher, Terri Seggio, was no nonsense. She shaped you into a young professional very fast. You were off-book before anybody, and you knew everybody else's roles and lines. You didn't have any theater before this, but when you walked onto the stage, you were Dorothy. I realized, *This is it.* I knew that day, this was it going forward, and we never had a plan B.

You were super smart. Honor roll student from day one. You could have gone into anything, lawyer, doctor... But after Dorothy all that went out the window, and I just saw you as an actress. I never thought about you going down any other road.

Maleah It is such a privileged experience to have parents who never forced me into a backup plan. Mom, being an immigrant from Belize, had more of a survival perspective on life. Even so, she saw her daughter's excellence as a kid and chose to trust them to become an artist—this abstract, scary, unknown thing. That makes me want to cry. It brings me a lot of joy, because my mom could have said, "You know what, Baby, that life doesn't always work. You should become a doctor. You should go into business." And I imagine, Dad, you work this blue-collar job your entire life, and to find out I want to be an artist, there maybe was a little thing in the back of your head that was like—

Steve Never, ever.

Maleah That's beautiful. That's beautiful to me.

Steve I love entertainment. I grew up on music. It touched my soul. I associate it with my family and times we had. Trips traveling down south with my Uncle Randolph, lying in the back of the station wagon, looking through the moon roof at a sky packed full of stars. Sam Cook on the radio, driving down to Virginia. Otis Redding on the eight-track. The click of the cartridge going into the player. It was already in me to be a part of it.

Maleah You wanted to be an artist as a young man, but you ended up doing other stuff. What makes a parent so willing to put aside their own dreams to support their child's aspirations?

Steve I didn't put aside my dreams. I'm still living them out through you. And I still wish I could sing like you.

Maleah I keep telling you that you just gotta come to me for the lessons, but you don't put aside the time. This is my last question. Would you say that the dream was realized? Would you say that it all paid off?

Steve Really? You're really asking me that? Yes. And this is only the start of the journey.

Maleah Every opportunity you had to support me, it was like, *I'm going to be the best cheerleader that she has, and I'm going to give her a standard of what it's like to be taken care of and supported and encouraged.* You are my world. You've always been great to me. And it's never taken in vain.

Maleah Joi Moon as Dorothy in *The Wizard of Oz*, with her father, Steve Moon

What we did at the Public, which was bad, was that he came into "Empire," and we had a silent scene of, *Do I accept him?* There was a dumb little show of, *Is it okay if I'm back?* and then resistance, and then finally a hug. We always knew it was on the lame side, so it was wonderful to be able to take a step back and find a better entry.

Kris Diaz, book writer
At the end of the show, Davis is showing back up, but we had to make sure that we didn't give the impression that it was all taken care of. It's not. Ali says a line that we found late in the Broadway rehearsal process, which is, "It's not all good, but it's alright." The idea is that this is a guy who's never going to be a perfect dad, but that him coming back to play with her is something.

In the same "Empire" scene, one more small change for Ali made an enormous dramaturgical difference.

Kris Diaz
We wanted Ali to embrace her community and embrace New York City, but even though her delivery of the song was super dynamic, the scene wasn't doing exactly what we wanted it to do. We finally realized it was because the story is about her learning to find her voice through the piano. So we had her play the piano while she sang, and now that moment shows exactly what we wanted: She understands what it means to express herself this way, and because of that, the next part of her life can start.

KALEIDOSCOPIC IMPACT

Although *Hell's Kitchen* was an immediate hit on Broadway, earning thirteen Tony nominations, the impact of the show can't be measured solely in ticket sales, awards, or glowing reviews. *Hell's Kitchen*'s success is also about how the show lifts spirits, opens doors, creates community, and celebrates all forms of art.

Chris Lee
You can find yourself in all these characters. That's what's so cool. When I was not on the stage, I got to watch, and I would walk away feeling like, "I could be a better person. I could judge less." It's funny that you would get that from a mother-daughter love story, but it's because you're absorbing this idea that everyone is more than just one thing. The reason that mom and daughter finally connect is because they see each other as more than just a stupid kid and an annoying overbearing mother. *Oh my gosh, there's so much more to you than that*. That's what it did for me.

Maleah Joi Moon as Ali with Chris Lee as Knuck during "Empire State of Mind"

Camille A. Brown (choreographer) and Robert Brill (scenic design) on opening night

Kecia Lewis on opening night

"I FEEL HONORED AND THANKFUL TO BE A PART OF SOMETHING THAT IS BRINGING SO MUCH JOY."

Maleah Joi Moon, actor (Ali)

Community is a theme in *Hell's Kitchen*, and it's such an important thing. Honestly, when I was in high school and seventeen like Ali, everything in life was about freedom and being independent. Then as you get older, you start to realize, *I do need people. I do need my parents, and I do need my teachers, and I can't do any of this by myself, and I don't want to.* Nobody wants to.

Aaron Lustbader

For me, working on this show has been glorious and affirming and something I'm very proud of. When I was first asked to put my hat in the ring for the job, I actually said no, and I said no a second time, too, because I had made a commitment with my husband. We'd just come back from the pandemic, and we had agreed to take it a little bit easier. Thankfully, the third time I was asked, I was explaining why I couldn't be considered, and my husband heard me on the phone. He said, "Are you saying no to Alicia Keys?" I said, "Yeah, because I promised you." And he said, "You can make an exception." I changed my answer immediately, and I'm so glad I did.

If you ask anyone who worked on this what was so special about it, anybody who doesn't answer "Alicia" to that question is on a different plane than I am. Alicia has produced the show while also being its central creative vision. Everybody who was invited onto this show was invited by her, and she cares about every detail. How is that social media post presented? How is the actor styled in it? What's the vibe? I also would say, up until working on *Hell's Kitchen*, I've never understood what the word "vibe" actually means, how all-encompassing it can be. But now I do. She is one of the single smartest people I've ever worked with.

Mandy Hackett

This show does not talk down to teenagers. It really puts it all out there: your fights with your mom, kissing a boy for the first time, falling in love, having sex, running away. I think that's why young people love this show so much: They feel like they're seeing themselves onstage.

As a mom of two daughters, I'm also the target audience. And if you're a mom, and you saw it with your friends or partner, you want to bring your kids back. You want to see it with your own mom. It has tentacles, it touches people.

One of the things I love the most about working in the theater is that if you have a show that works, it's the truest reflection of the artists making it, and Alicia is so full of hope and optimism. She is a force for positivity and transformation. We talked a lot about transformation when we were making the show, that it's not easy for Ali. She loses someone she loves. She gets hurt by her dad. She gets hurt by her mom. But at the end of the show, by the time you hit "Empire," it is so full of hope and positivity and building your community and the power of the arts to help you move forward.

I think that's why the theater transforms people. It can leave you feeling uplifted and positive without being sappy—it's earned.

Monet, associate director

My policy in making art is that I want to make great things with good people for the people. I wholeheartedly believe that that is everything that Alicia is doing, and it's everything that Michael is doing. I feel honored and thankful to be a part of something that is bringing so much joy, because it's hard out here. No matter how many times I've seen the show, which is probably second-most next to the mixer, Sean Woods, it's such a pleasure to be around the audience, seeing the people who are coming. It's a joy to see so many Black people at the theater. I feel very honored that people spend their hard-earned money to come see the show.

So many memories are being made. You get all these moms and daughters. I can't even handle it. When I have friends come, I say, "Here are tissues. I don't want to ruin it for you, but brace yourself." I see the big families or the girlfriends who come. Young people come, and all they're doing is looking at 'Riq and Q and Jessica and Tiny, and I love that for them. And then you have Miss Liza Jane; if you're lucky in your life, you've had someone like her.

It's really cliché to say there's something for everybody, but when you make full characters, everybody has someone to love, everybody has someone to

A SHOWER OF FLOWERS

Kecia Lewis accepting her Tony for Best Featured Actress in a Musical

Maleah Joi Moon with their Tony for Best Actress in a Musical

2024–2025 AWARDS

Tony Award
Best Actress in a Musical
Maleah Joi Moon

Tony Award
Best Featured Actress in a Musical
Kecia Lewis

Lucille Lortel Award
Outstanding Featured Performer in a Musical
Kecia Lewis

Drama League Award
Outstanding Production of a Musical

Outer Critics Circle Award
Outstanding Featured Performer in a Broadway Musical
Kecia Lewis

Drama Desk Award
Outstanding Projection and Video Design
Peter Nigrini

Drama Desk Award
Outstanding Lead Performance in a Musical
Maleah Joi Moon

Chita Rivera Award
Outstanding Choreography in a Broadway Show
Camille A. Brown

Theatre World Award
Maleah Joi Moon

Grammy Award
Best Musical Theater Album
Original Broadway Cast

Alicia with the *Hell's Kitchen* Grammy on top of the Empire State Building

The cast performing "Empire State of Mind"

TOMMY
TOMMY

"IT'S CRAZY TO THINK THAT IT ALL STARTED WITH THAT LITTLE SPARK OF FRUSTRATION, BUT A SPARK IS HOW YOU MAKE FIRE."

identify with. While we cover some challenging things in the show, the net positive is joy and hope.

Michael Greif
I go to the show a lot, and you get a sense that many people are experiencing musical theater for the first time. Lots of young people and lots of families. It's music they want to hear that has brought them, but once they're there, it's a story people can really get behind. They see what great choreography is and they see what musical theater storytelling is. It's a lot of people's introduction to musical theater, which makes me very, very happy.

Alicia Keys
I'm so proud of what this show means to people. I look around and it's a dream come true. I love how people leave the theater after the show. You're laughing, you're crying, you're calling your loved ones.

Behind the scenes of the Broadway run, Alicia worked with Alexa Smith and Foresight Theatrical management company's Devon Miller to design a fellowship program that gave talented and underrepresented young people high-level exposure to the world of musical theater. More than 2,500 people applied for ten spots, and each artistic department head, from choreographer Camille A. Brown to sound designer Gareth Owen, personally interviewed the fellows they chose. Fellows didn't just observe from the sidelines; they were tasked with real duties and responsibilities. And Alicia's team coordinated with a labor union so that the fellows could be paid for their time—a key aspect of the program, since unpaid opportunities can take many qualified candidates out of the running.

Alicia is forever exploring and expanding ways to use her voice. When she uses it to express her imagination and artistry, we end up with a musical like *Hell's Kitchen*. But she also uses her platform to show love for her greater community, humankind. In every facet of the show's conception and execution, she has opened doors.

Alicia Keys
I remember that day the fellows first came to a rehearsal. I saw that group of beautiful, talented people, full of their own dreams, and thought, *This is the stuff we want to add to the theater world. This is how we want to make it different and new.*

Adam Blackstone, music supervisor and co-orchestrator
Alicia was huge on representation for women and people of color. I'm very proud of the crew and the band that we have in the string section. I have two African American horn players. Asian descent all over the pit, women stage managers, women of color in the actual show. Alicia was adamant about being inclusive, and sometimes it was hard. It was hard to find a mature Black woman on the keys to represent Miss Liza Jane, because Broadway has always been a hand-me-down type of place. I think Alicia is giving so many people new opportunities. We're not necessarily the first show to do this, but we have definitely been an impactful one.

Lily Ling, music director
We're surrounded by so many amazing women with Monet and Alicia and Kecia. We've been able to do so much outreach and mentorship and education. Many of the substitute musicians are making their Broadway debut, and we've set them up for success. We're able to plant seeds for the next generation or support people who have been overlooked, like Miss Aziza. To me, that is truly the gift of *Hell's Kitchen*.

Alicia Keys
It was a long time coming to bring this show to life, but it's 1000% been worth it. This show tells the truth about everything that helps us make our dreams come true—how much we rely on the love and inspiration of people around us, how much we are a part of the places we come from, and how much we have to listen to the music inside our hearts. It's crazy to think that it all started with that little spark of frustration, but a spark is how you make fire.

Terria Joseph, Oprah Winfrey, Alicia Keys, Michelle Obama, Gayle King, and Swizz Beatz on opening night

HITTING THE STREETS

Alicia Keys's *Hell's Kitchen* is a love letter to New York, and its audiences have answered with laughter, tears, and dancing in their seats. In every performance, from the star-studded Broadway opening to special schoolkid audiences and after-show talkbacks, the show has delivered a message of what it means to love people for who they are, what it means to be part of something larger than oneself, and what it means to dream. In both promotions and outreach, the company has spilled out into the city's streets and schools and stadiums. Actors, dancers, and musicians have generously participated in talkbacks and halftime shows. They've sung on subway platforms and danced in parades. Time and again, they've set the city on fire.

The success of the fellows' program inspired Alicia to start the not-for-profit Kaleidoscope Dreams Foundation. The foundation's vision of equity, diversity, and inclusion is expansive, including community engagement, in-school residencies, artist grants, subsidized performances, and tech-theater intensives. Kaleidoscope Dreams will support a new round of fellows for the national *Hell's Kitchen* tour that travels to more than thirty cities across the country from Orlando to San Francisco beginning in the fall of 2025—and will continue to create opportunities with other partners down the line. Among Alicia's longtime concerns is the Keep a Child Alive (KCA) Foundation, which she cofounded in 2003. KCA supports community-based initiatives to uplift children and families affected by HIV in Africa, Southern Europe, and Asia. Alicia saw a throughline between *Hell's Kitchen* and KCA. "*Hell's Kitchen* is about a seventeen-year-old girl trying to find her way in NYC," she says. "Both *Hell's Kitchen* and Keep a Child Alive believe that every child in the world should have the opportunity to thrive." Since the show's opening at the Shubert Theatre, one dollar from every ticket sold has been donated to KCA. Ticket sales, combined with donations, resulted in more than a million dollars donated after just the first six months.

Hell's Kitchen is an exquisitely crafted and thoroughly entertaining theater experience, but it's also a show about opening doors that has and will always, in its very essence, open actual doors: showcasing new talent, bringing new audiences to musical theater, and creating new ways for people to show up for each other.

Alicia Keys and Serena Williams at the US Open after the *Hell's Kitchen* cast performed

The cast performing in the 59th Street/Columbus Circle subway station in Manhattan

The *Hell's Kitchen* cast performing "Empire State of Mind" during a Knicks game at Madison Square Garden

Alicia with some of the *Hell's Kitchen* fellows: Shivanna Sooknanan, Tanashua Harris Santiago, Amiah McGinty, and Zoë Elizabeth Lillis

PLAZA

Each page of this book - Every Thoughtful word and every stunning photo - tells the story of a dream That became a reality. My dream was to see something on broadway That felt like The people and experiences I knew growing up. I wanted to share a story That hadn't been told.

PUTTING TOGETHER This book allowed me to reflect on every part of That journey, The moments of discovery and inspiration and The extrodinary gift of collaboration.

Hell's Kitchen Celebrates Those relationships and places That inspire us to come into our full potential. My biggest wish is That everyone Can have a mentor figure as influential as Miss Liza Jane and a parent figure as fiercely loving as Jersey. I Hope, after reading This book, you'll recognize The people who've lifted you up along The way and That you'll do The same for Someone else.

Get out, Dream big, And make a difference!!

IMAGE CREDITS

All photographs are copyright © their respective sources.

Cover art: Brand design by AKA; 6: Marc J Franklin; 8: Russell Kord ARCHIVE/Alamy Stock Photo; 10: Roger Rowlett/Wikimedia Commons; 11: Courtesy of Alicia Keys; 12–13 (background): Elvert Barnes/Flickr; 13 (topmost row, left): Diane Rooney/Wikimedia Commons; 13 (topmost row, middle): Amy Martin Photography/ Wikimedia Commons; 13 (topmost row, right): David Shankbone/ Wikimedia Commons; 13 (second row from top, left): Greg2600/ Wikimedia Commons; 13 (second row from top, middle): Gage Skidmore/Wikimedia Commons; 13 (second row from top, right): Super Festivals/Wikimedia Commons; 13 (second row from bottom, left): Frantogian/Wikimedia Commons; 13 (second row from bottom, right): Eva Rinaldi/Wikimedia Commons; 13 (bottommost row, left): Embajada de EEUU en la Argentina (US Embassy of Argentina)/ Wikimedia Commons; 13 (bottommost row, right): Orlando Fernandez/Wikimedia Commons; 14: Michaelah Reynolds; 14–15: Ramon Rivas; 16: Ramon Rivas; 18: Tom Copi/Getty; 19 (top): Marc J Franklin; 19 (middle right): Phil O'Brien; 19 (bottom left): Johnny Nuñez; 19 (bottom right): Doug Grimes III at DxG Studios; 20–23: Ramon Rivas; 24: Anton Martynov; 25: Ramon Rivas; 26: Glen Frieson; 27 (top): Courtesy of Alicia Keys; 27 (bottom): Ramon Rivas; 28: Marc J Franklin; 30: Marc J Franklin; 31: Ramon Rivas; 33 (topmost row): Courtesy of The Public Theater; 33 (bottom): Joseph Augstein; 34–35: Ramon Rivas; 36: Marc J Franklin; 37: Paul Archuleta/Getty; 38: Michaelah Reynolds; 39: Marc J Franklin; 40: Ramon Rivas; 41: Marc J Franklin; 42–45: Ramon Rivas; 47: Angela Orellana; 48: Jenny Anderson/Stringer; 49–51: Marc J Franklin; 52: Nicolas Wheelehon; 53: Ramon Rivas; 56: Ramon Rivas; 58–65: Ramon Rivas; 66: Marc J Franklin; 67: Marc J Franklin; 68–69: Michaelah Reynolds; 70: Ramon Rivas; 71: Alonzo Boldin/ Zo Photography; 72: Gareth Owens; 73: Michaelah Reynolds; 75 (top): Ramon Rivas; 75 (middle and bottom): Marc J Franklin; 77: Lily Ling; 79: Marc J Franklin; 80–81: Ramon Rivas; 84: Michaelah Reynolds; 88–89: Marc J Franklin; 91–95: Marc J Franklin; 97–107: Marc J Franklin; 109: Marc J Franklin; 111–129: Marc J Franklin; 131: Marc J Franklin: 134–137: Marc J Franklin; 139–147: Marc J Franklin; 149–150: Marc J Franklin; 152–161: Marc J Franklin; 163–174: Marc J Franklin; 176: Marc J Franklin; 178–179: Marc J Franklin; 181: Courtesy of Dede Ayite, Hochi Asiatico, Eric Wintering, and Cathy Parrott; 182 (top): Courtesy of Dede Ayite, Hochi Asiatico, Eric Wintering, and Cathy Parrott; 182 (bottom, left and right): Eric Winterling; 183 (top): Courtesy of Dede Ayite, Hochi Asiatico, Eric Wintering, and Cathy Parrott; 183 (bottom): Eric Winterling; 184–185: Marc J Franklin; 186: Whitney Browne; 187: Ramon Rivas; 188–189: Marc J Franklin; 190–191: Ramon Rivas; 193: Marc J Franklin; 195: Michael Clifton; 196: Marc J Franklin; 198: Marc J Franklin; 200: Peter Nigrini; 201: Marc J Franklin; 202–203: Peter Nigrini; 204: Marc J Franklin; 205: Robert Brill; 207–208: Ramon Rivas; 209: Marc J Franklin; 212: Marc J Franklin; 214: Michaelah Reynolds; 216: Marc J Franklin; 217: Michaelah Reynolds; 219: Katrena Wize; 220: Courtesy of Kenneth and Linda Diaz; 221: Courtesy of Steve and Maleah Joi Moon; 222: Marc J Franklin; 223–224: Michaelah Reynolds; 226 (top): Theo Wargo/Getty; 226 (bottom): Cindy Ord/ Getty; 227: Laurel Hinton; 228–229: Marc J Franklin; 231: Flo Ngala; 233 (top left): Jennifer Pottheiser/USTA; 233 (top right): Joana Meurkens; 233 (center right): Laurel Hinton; 233 (bottom): Ramon Rivas; 234–235: Marc J Franklin; 236: Ramon Rivas; Back cover: Ramon Rivas.

SONG CREDITS

"LOVE LOOKS BETTER"
Written by Alicia J. Augello-Cook, Ryan B. Tedder, Lorrance Levar Dopson, Noel Zancanella
Copyright © 2020 Universal Music Corp., Lellow Prod., Inc., Write Me a Song Publishing, Songs of Patriot Games, Blastronaut Publishing, Peermusic III Ltd., Songs of Volume Ventures, and Blue Nike Publishing
All rights for Lellow Prod., Inc. administered by Universal Music Corp.
All rights for Write Me a Song Publishing administered by Downtown Global Two
All rights for Songs of Patriot Games and Blastronaut Publishing administered by Downtown Music Publishing.
Used by permission of Peermusic III, Ltd. o/b/o Songs of Volume Ventures and Blue Nike Publishing
All rights reserved used by permission
Reprinted by permission of Hal Leonard LLC

"AUTHORS OF FOREVER"
Words and music by Alicia J. Augello-Cook, Jonny Coffer, Johnny McDaid
Copyright © 2020 Universal Music Corp., Lellow Prod., Inc., B-Unique Music Limited, and Sony/ATV Songs LLC
All rights for Lellow Prod., Inc. administered by Universal Music Corp.
All rights for B-Unique Music Limited administered by Songs of Kobalt Music Publishing
All rights for Sony/ATV Songs LLC administered by Sony Music Publishing LLC, 424 Church Street, Suite 1200, Nashville, TN 37219
Reprinted by permission of Hal Leonard LLC
All rights reserved used by permission

"EMPIRE STATE OF MIND PT 2"
Words and music by Alicia J. Augello-Cook, Bert Keyes, Sylvia Robinson, Shawn C. Carter, Angela Ann Hunte, Janet Andrea Sewell, Alexander William Shuckburgh
Copyright © 2009 Universal Music Corp., Lellow Productions, Inc., Gambi Music, Inc., Twenty Nine Black Music, Emi Foray Music, J. Sewell Publishing, EMI April Music Inc., Carter Boys Music, and KMR II GT Publishing Limited
All rights for Lellow Productions administered by Universal Music Corp.
All rights for Gambi Music, Inc. and Twenty Nine Black Music administered by Songs of Universal, Inc.
All rights for Emi Foray Music, J. Sewell Publishing, EMI April Music Inc., and Carter Boys Music administered by Sony Music Publishing LLC, 424 Church Street, Suite 1200, Nashville, TN 37219
All rights for KMR II GT Publishing Limited administered by Songs of Kobalt Music Publishing
All rights reserved used by permission
Contains elements of "Love on a Two-Way Street" (Keyes/Robinson) © 1970 Twenty Nine Black Music and Gambi Music Inc.
Reprinted by permission of Hal Leonard LLC

"FALLIN'"
Words and music by Alicia J. Augello-Cook
Copyright © Universal Music Corp. on behalf of itself and Lellow Prod., Inc. (ASCAP)
All rights reserved used by permission

"GIRL ON FIRE"
Words and music by Alicia J. Augello-Cook, Onika Tanya Maraj, Jeffrey Nath Bhasker, Salaam Remi, Billy Squier
Copyright © 2012 Universal Music Corp., Lellow Productions Inc., Money Mack Music, Universal Music Works, Ken & Barbie Music, Sony Music Publishing (US) LCC, Way Above Music, Songs of the Knight, and Analog Meta Verse
All rights for Lellow Productions Inc. administered by Universal Music Corp.
All rights for Money Mack Music administered by Songs of Universal, Inc. All rights for Ken & Barbie Music administered by Universal Music Works

All rights for Sony Music Publishing (US) LLC and Way Above Music administered by Sony Music Publishing (US) LLC, 424 Church Street, Suite 1200, Nashville, TN 37219
All rights for Songs of the Knight administered by Spirit Two Music, Inc.
All rights for Analog Meta Verse administered by Warner-Tamerlane Publishing Corp.
All rights reserved used by permission
Reprinted by permission of Hal Leonard LLC
Used by permission of Alfred Music

"THE GOSPEL"
Words and music by Alicia J. Augello-Cook, Dennis David Coles, Kasseem Dean, Robert F. Diggs, Lamont Hawkins, Corey Woods, Mark Christopher Batson, Shawn Martin
Copyright © 2016 Universal Music Corp., Lellow Prod., Inc., Swizz Beats, Universal Music Careers, Wu Tang Anthems, Universal Music-MGB Songs, Dynamic Reality Music, and Shawn Martin Publishing Designee
All rights for Lellow Prod., Inc. and Swizz Beats administered by Universal Music Corp.
All rights for Wu Tang Anthems administered by Songs of Universal, Inc.
All rights for Dynamic Reality Music administered by Songs of Kobalt Music Publishing
All rights reserved used by permission
Reprinted by permission of Hal Leonard LLC

"GRAMERCY PARK"
Words and music by Alicia J. Augello-Cook, Samuel Elliot Roman, James John Napier
Copyright © 2020 Universal Music Corp., Lellow Prod., Inc., Songs of Universal, Inc., Songs of Roc Nation Music, and Concord Sisl Ltd.
All rights for Lellow Prod., Inc. administered by Universal Music Corp.
All rights for Songs of Roc Nation Music administered by Songs of Universal, Inc.
All rights on behalf of Concord Sisl Ltd. administered by Concord Lane c/o Concord Music Publishing
All rights reserved used by permission
Reprinted by permission of Hal Leonard LLC

"HALLELUJAH"
Words and music by Alicia J. Augello-Cook, James John Napier
Copyright © 2016 Universal Music Corp., Lellow Productions, Inc. and Concord Sisl Limited
All rights for Lellow Prod., Inc. administered by Universal Music Corp.
All rights for Concord Sisl Limited administered by Concord Lane c/o Concord Music Publishing
All rights reserved used by permission
Reprinted by permission of Hal Leonard LLC

"HEARTBURN"
Words and music by Alicia J. Augello-Cook, Candice Clotiel Nelson, Walter Worth Milsap, Timothy Z. Mosley
Copyright © 2003 Universal Music Corp., Lellow Productions, Inc., Bootleggers Stop, Phoenix Rose Music Publishing, Flight Thru Music, EMI April Music Inc., Conjunction Music Publishing, and WC Music Corp.
© 2004 WB Music Corp. (ASCAP), EMI April Music Inc. (ASCAP), Lellow Prod., Inc. (ASCAP), Conjunction Music Publishing (ASCAP), and Bread Winner Entertainment Publishing Company (ASCAP)
All rights for Lellow Productions and Bootleggers Stop administered by Universal Music Corp.
All rights for Phoenix Rose Music Publishing, Flight Thru Music, EMI April Music Inc., and Conjunction Music Publishing administered by Sony Music Publishing LLC, 424 Church Street, Suite 1200, Nashville, TN 37219
All rights reserved used by permission
Reprinted by permission of Hal Leonard LLC
Used by permission of Alfred Music

"IF I AIN'T GOT YOU"
Words and music by Alicia J. Augello-Cook
(Copyright © Universal Music Corp. on behalf of itself and Lellow Prod., Inc. (ASCAP)

"KALEIDOSCOPE"
Words and music by Alicia J. Augello-Cook, Ben Diehl, Breyan Stanley Isaac, Gamal Kosh Lewis
Copyright © Universal Music Corp. on behalf of itself and Lellow Prod., Inc. (ASCAP)
© 2024 Billions Enterprises (BMI)
All rights on behalf of Billions Enterprises administered by Warner-Tamerlane Publishing Corp.
All rights reserved
Used by permission of Alfred Music

"LIKE WATER (ORIGINALS)"
Words and music by Alicia J. Augello-Cook, Mark Batson, Sia Kate I. Furler
Copyright © 2021 Universal Music Corp., Lellow Prod., Inc., Pineapple Lasagne, and Bat Future Music
All rights for Lellow Prod., Inc. administered by Universal Music Corp.
All rights for Pineapple Lasagne administered by Sony Music Publishing LLC, 424 Church Street, Suite 1200, Nashville, TN 37219
All rights for Bat Future Music administered by Songs of Kobalt Music Publishing
All rights reserved used by permission
Reprinted by permission of Hal Leonard LLC

"LIKE YOU'LL NEVER SEE ME AGAIN"
Words and music by Alicia J. Augello-Cook, Kerry D. Brothers Jr.
Copyright © 2007 Universal Music Corp., Lellow Prod., Inc., and EMI April Music Inc.
All rights for Lellow Prod., Inc. administered by Universal Music Corp.
All rights for EMI April Music Inc. administered by Sony Music Publishing LLC, 424 Church Street, Suite 1200, Nashville, TN 37219
All rights reserved used by permission
Reprinted by permission of Hal Leonard LLC

"NO ONE"
Words and music by Alicia J. Augello-Cook, George Michael Harry, Kerry D. Brothers Jr.
Copyright © 2007 Universal Music Corp., Lellow Prod., Inc., D. Harry Productions, and EMI April Music Inc.
All rights for Lellow Productions, Inc. and D. Harry Productions administered by Universal Music Corp.
All rights for EMI April Music Inc. administered by Sony Music Publishing (US) LLC, 424 Church Street, Suite 1200, Nashville, TN 37219
All rights reserved used by permission
Reprinted by permission of Hal Leonard LLC

"NOT EVEN THE KING"
Words and music by Alicia J. Augello-Cook, Emeli Sande
Copyright © 2012 Universal Music Corp., Lellow Prod., Inc., and Stellar Songs Limited
All rights for Lellow Prod., Inc. administered by Universal Music Corp.
All rights for Stellar Songs Limited administered by Sony Music Publishing LLC, 424 Church Street, Suite 1200, Nashville, TN 37219
All rights reserved used by permission
Reprinted by permission of Hal Leonard LLC

"PAWN IT ALL"
Words and music by Alicia J. Augello-Cook, Kasseem Dean, Mark Christopher Batson, Harold Spencer Jr. Lilly
Copyright © 2016 Universal Music Corp., Lellow Productions, Inc., Swizz Beats, Uncle Bobby Music, Hipgnosis SFH I Limited, and Bat Future Music
All rights for Lellow Prod., Inc. and Swizz Beats administered by Universal Music Corp.
All rights for Uncle Bobby Music administered by Sony Music Publishing LLC, 424 Church Street, Suite 1200, Nashville, TN 37219
All rights for Hipgnosis SFH I Limited and Bat Future Music administered by Songs of Kobalt Music Company
All rights reserved used by permission
Reprinted by permission of Hal Leonard LLC

"PERFECT WAY TO DIE"
Words and music by Alicia J. Augello-Cook, Coleridge Tillman

"RIVER, THE"
Words and music by Alicia J. Augello-Cook, Johnny McDaid

"SEVENTEEN"
Words and music by Alicia J. Augello-Cook

"TEENAGE LOVE AFFAIR"
Words and music by Alicia J. Augello-Cook, Jo Bridges, Carl Mitchell Hampton, Tom Nixon, Matt Kahane, Harold Spencer Jr. Lilly

Contains sample of "Girl I Love You" by Carl Hampton, Jo Bridges, and Tom Nixon

"UN-THINKABLE (I'M READY)"
Words and music by Alicia J. Augello-Cook, Aubrey Drake Graham, Kerry D. Brothers Jr., Noah James Shebib

"WORK ON IT"
Words and music by Alicia J. Augello-Cook, Pharrell L. Williams

"YOU DON'T KNOW MY NAME"
Words and music by Alicia J. Augello-Cook, J. R. Bailey, Mel Kent, Harold Spencer Jr. Lilly, Kanye Omari West, Kenneth Williams